To Bill Soccorsy

Keep Writing

David F. Trottier

11-30-02

DR. FORMAT

ANSWERS YOUR QUESTIONS

by David Trottier

First Dave Trottier Edition
10 9 8 7 6 5 4 3 2

Library of Congress Cataloging-in-Publication Data

Trottier, David
Dr. Format Answers Your Questions / by David Trottier
p. cm.
Includes index.
1. Motion picture authorship. 2. Television authorship.
I. Title
808.2'3   2002093850 LCCN

ISBN: 1-885655-08-8

Cover design by Bob Nicholl

Printed in the United States of America

Dave Trottier
4456 Manchester St.
Cedar Hills, UT 84062

PURPOSE AND CONTENTS

The purpose of this book is to provide you with guidance on very specific formatting and spec screenplay writing topics. Understanding formatting and spec writing is a necessary key to crafting a readable and saleable script. This book shows you how to turn the key.

This book contains two sections:

1. An updated version of all of my *Dr. Format* **columns** published in *scr(i)pt* magazine from 1997 through 2002, plus two articles on screenwriting.

2. A very clear and thorough **index**, beginning on page 111. Use this index to find explanations of every possible formatting situation.

For information on either *scr(i)pt* magazine or my services, see page 119.

Keep writing,
Dave Trottier
www.keepwriting.com
dave@keepwriting.com

DR. FORMAT COLUMNS
scr(i)pt magazine
1997 through 2002

plus two articles on screenwriting

First Dr. Format Column
February, 1997

It seems like every week I come across some new rule that someone is touting as the latest in script format. I get regular calls from writers asking about this fine point or that.

This column will answer your formatting questions. In doing so, I hope to take the mystery out of formatting, dispel the confusion that surrounds it, explode common formatting myths, and help you make that all-important first impression with your script.

What is the purpose of formatting?

Its purpose is to present a story in readable form so that the reader will recommend your script to higher-ups. *Readable form* means the reader can easily visualize the action of the story, hear the characters in his or her head, and feel the emotion that underpins the story. That means the writing must be clear, moving, and easy-to-follow.

Many writers believe this means including camera angles, editing instructions, and other technical directions. This is exactly the wrong thing to do. Why? Because it intrudes on "the read." Which is more interesting to read? *ESTABLISHING SHOT - NEW YORK* or *The skyline of New York City sparkles in the sunlight.* The second version is clearer, more easily visualized, and easier to read.

Another purpose of formatting is to provide a generally-accepted standard framework in which to tell a story, not direct the movie. That constantly-evolving standard includes three basic sections:

1) Headings, including the master scene heading, 2) Narrative description, and 3) Dialogue. You are familiar with these, but do you understand the fine points of formatting that make a difference?

Formatting is not one of the profundities of the universe. It is simple and straight-forward. On the other hand, formatting is more than just a few rules about margins and tabs, it is a style guide to writing a salable script. To understand formatting is to understand screenwriting.

Working with Foreign Languages

QUESTION
If I have a conversation in Chinese as well as English, do I use the dreaded wrylies to define Chinese and English? Also, in defining film reality, can I avoid the language barrier by having my Chinese scenes in English?

ANSWER
First, let me explain the question. The writer refers to "dreaded wrylies." *Wrylies* are the parentheticals that sometimes appear before dialogue. The term developed because so many beginners use the term *wryly* to describe their characters' dialogue.

```
                    JOHN
               (wryly)
          The night is still young,
          Cupcake.
```

And so the term *wryly* was born. The reason they are "dreaded" is because writers are encouraged to avoid their use. Only use a wryly when the subtext of the dialogue is not otherwise clear.

In working with other languages, realize there is one central principle: Write your script in the language of the eventual reader. In other words, avoid foreign languages. If a character speaks in Chinese, do not write the dialogue out in Chinese characters unless the eventual reader is Chinese. Simply write the line as follows.

```
          JOHN
       (in Chinese)
  The night is still young,
  Cupcake.
```

If the characters speak in Chinese throughout an entire scene, then make a clear statement in the narrative description that all the dialogue in the scene will be spoken in Chinese; then, write it out in English so the reader can understand it. But this begs the question: How will the audience know what is being said? They won't. That's why one option is to write a line or two in Chinese for flavor, and allow the characters speak in English so that the audience will understand what is going on.

There is another alternative--subtitles. If you want English subtitles to appear on the screen while the characters speak in Chinese, then include a special note in the narrative description.

```
NOTE:  THE DIALOGUE IN THIS SCENE IS
SPOKEN IN CHINESE AND IS SUBTITLED IN
ENGLISH.
```

Then, simply write the dialogue out in English. After the scene ends, write:

```
END OF SUBTITLES
```

There are other ways to indicate subtitles, but the above is the simplest and less intrusive.

A SUPER question

QUESTION
When writing a screenplay, is it the writer who writes the text that appears on the screen? I'm thinking of *X-files* and *Clear and Present Danger*.

ANSWER
The *text* you refer to is actually a SUPERIMPOSITION. You *superimpose* a title card or legend over the image that we see. The term *superimpose* is generally shortened to SUPER in a spec script. Here's an example.

```
EXT. HOSPITAL - NIGHT

EMTs rush a patient out of an ambulance and
into the hospital.

SUPER: "Bethesda Medical Hospital."

Scully's car comes to a quick stop.    She
steps out with her cellular.

                    SCULLY
               (into cellular)
          Mulder?  Are you there?
```

Please note that I followed the heading (or slug line) with a sentence of description. You must first give the audience a visual image before presenting the SUPER that will appear over that image.

If you'd like, here is an alternative expression for a SUPER:

```
The words "BETHESDA MEDICAL HOSPITAL" spell
out across the lower left of the screen.
```

The unkindest CUT TO of all

QUESTION
Someone told me, "If I submit my script using the CUT TO editing direction like William Goldman does, my script is going to get laughed straight into the trash can." On the other hand, some screenwriting books promote the use of CUT TO. Is there a proper time and place for CUT TO, or should I omit the use of the term altogether?

ANSWER
First of all, established writers can do what they please and Goldman (one of my heroes) uses the CUT TO after virtually every scene and shot. It's excessive by spec script standards.

Although a screenwriting book may recommend use of the CUT TO, it will not suggest that you use it a la William Goldman. However, in the evolution of *spec* format, the CUT TO is seldom used today. Look at the copyright notice of any book recommending its use and note how long it's been since that book was written; also, make sure the book is not demonstrating *shooting* script format.

In writing a *spec* script today, avoid editing directions like CUT TO, DISSOLVE TO, WIPE TO, MATCH CUT, etc. However, there are times to use them. Here is Trottier Axiom #7 to guide you: *Use an editing direction when it is absolutely necessary to understand the story, or when its use helps link two scenes in a way that creates humor or improves continuity.* Under that rule of thumb, I find myself using editing directions about twice every 120 pages.

In the following example, Bruno stands next to a bed with a canopy overhead. Lying on the bed is Alice. Bruno has resisted her verbal advances up until now, so she tries a new approach.

                    ALICE
          Here, let me give you a
          little candy sampler of
          what's waiting for you on
          the honeymoon.

She swings her legs up, throws a scissors
lock around Bruno's neck and flips him
onto the bed, then pounces on him like a
professional wrestler. His eyes grow wide
in terror.

                              CUT TO:

INT. BEDROOM - THE NEXT MORNING

Bruno's leg dangles from the canopy. He
blissfully sings an Italian love song.

Alice, below him, lays back on the bed with
her hands behind her head, calmly smoking a
cigar.

The purpose of the CUT TO here is to provide continuity
between the two scenes. The CUT TO also sets up the visual
punch line--it links the *before* with the *after*. Thus, we have a
special *story* reason to use it.

Keep in mind that in virtually all scene transitions, one scene
ends, followed by the heading for the next scene. The CUT TO
is nearly always understood and does not need to be written. In
short, let the editor do the editing and you do the writing.

SING FOR YOUR SUPPER

QUESTION
I am currently polishing a script that includes old song lyrics and improvisational rap in the dialogue. The parenthetical direction (i.e., rapping, singing) will probably work in most cases, but seems overused because of the volume of lyrical dialogue. I am considering four formatting options: 1) italicizing the lyrics, 2) underscoring, 3) using poetry-style layout (as opposed to wraparound text), and 4) slash marks (/) to convey lyrical rhythm. I can't seem to find a formatting rule to cover this. Help!

ANSWER
The reason you cannot find a formatting rule is because you are not supposed to include songs in a spec script. It's best not to quote any songs to which you don't own the rights. Doing so creates a legal roadblock to selling your script because the producer must obtain the rights to use the songs.

If the song is in the public domain, then you may use the lyrics. However, resist the temptation of using a song in a script unless the song has a powerful *story* purpose. When an agent or producer sees song lyrics in a script, they generally react negatively.

If the songs (or "improvisational rap") are original to you, including them in your script still adds an obstacle to the selling process. It means that the producer must not only love your script but the music/lyrics you wrote for it as well. And maybe he or she will.

If you must include song lyrics, use the parentheticals you mention, and use slash marks to separate the lines. Slash marks are acceptable for poetry and lyrics. The following is by Ogden Nash.

```
                OG
           (rapping)
     I don't think I'll ever see/
     A billboard lovely as a tree/
     Indeed, the tree I'll not see
     at all/ If the billboard
     doesn't fall.
```

Remember that a spec script should focus primarily on a great story. Tell a great story, and you'll be singing all the way to the bank.

DAYDREAM BELIEVER

QUESTION
If a character is listening to someone talking, and the character drifts off into a daydream or fantasy, how do you set it up?

ANSWER
Handle this the way you would a flashback. First, create a transitional device to slip us into the daydream. In the *Casablanca* flashback, we move toward the cigarette smoke and DISSOLVE to Paris. But a transition could easily be signaled with a word of dialogue or an action. Here's an example.

```
Mary listens to the voices behind the
door. They fade as she looks away.

MARY'S DAYDREAM
```

Describe the daydream. Then:

```
BACK TO SCENE
```

And continue with the original scene with Mary at the door.

If you have a special location in mind that you want to emphasize, write it as follows:

```
INT. AFRICAN JUNGLE -- MARY'S DAYDREAM
```

Or

```
MARY'S DAYDREAM -- AFRICAN JUNGLE
```

And then after the scene ends:

```
END OF DAYDREAM
```

```
INT. HALLWAY
```

...Or wherever the original scene took place.

Keep in mind that a spec script must be visually clear. The reader must be able to easily visualize the action and movement.

HOW WIDE IS A LINE?

QUESTION
I recently bought formatting software. The dialogue width (between the left margin of the speech and the right margin of the speech] seems to be wider than in most screenplays I've purchased and read. Can you tell me how wide a line of dialogue should be before it wraps around to the next line? It seems about 32-36 characters is proper width, but I've read it should be much shorter.

ANSWER
The ideal is three inches, but you can stretch that to about 3½ inches max. That gives you a range of about 30-35 characters per line (assuming you are using a standard 10 characters-per-inch font such as Courier or New Courier 12 point).

EXECUTIVE READERS AND READER READERS

QUESTION
I've read that executives and readers don't read narration, only dialogue. Is this accurate? If so, what's the best way to convey the action of the screenplay?

ANSWER
You have named two very different types of readers. A *reader* reader (the official term is *story analyst*) is someone who is paid (usually a pittance) to read scripts and write coverages. A *coverage* consists of a two-page synopsis (approximately) plus an evaluation of the script, along with the story analyst's recommendations. In order to write the coverage, the story analyst (reader) must read the script. So generally speaking, a professional reader reads both the narration and the dialogue.

An executive or producer usually does not read a script until he or she has a coverage. If the coverage is favorable, the executive or producer may read the script, or portions thereof, to see if he or she agrees with the opinion of the reader. Some Hollywood types read dialogue only, some read just a few pages, and some read the script like a professional reader. Some have law backgrounds or otherwise have little experience with screenplay form. Others have been in the business their entire lives.

In any case, you want to write narration that's lean. When any reader sees large blocks of black ink, he or she is likely to black out. You want to write narration that presents clear images and clear actions. Only include what is necessary to move the story forward. As a general rule, paragraphs of narration should not exceed four lines. And each paragraph should focus on one main image or one beat of action.

Let's examine the following poorly written narrative.

```
EXT. TRAIN - DAY

We see the skyline of New York from a
train.  Painted on the side of it are
words that say, Brooklyn Railroad.  It's
going very fast and has a gray look to it.

INT. TRAIN - DAY

Inside the train are all kinds of
commuters.  They are from every age and
ethnic group and they fill the train car
clean up.  They are all headed to work in
New York City as can be plainly seen from
their working clothes.  A bunch of them
cannot find seats and must stand.  One of
them is SALLY STANWICK, who has piercing
blue eyes and long, flowing locks of
blonde hair.  She is in her mid twenties
and is wearing a silk blouse with a pink
sweater over it and a plain black cotton
skirt.  She senses someone behind her and
turns to see a young man giving her the
eye and smiling at her in a very peculiar
way.
```

Here we have the first two paragraphs of a screenplay written by one of my clients (before he became a client). These big blocks of black ink are guaranteed to discourage any reader. Let's see if we can't whittle it down a little while being specific in describing images and actions.

```
FADE IN:

A speeding silver train races down the
tracks towards Manhattan. A sign on the
train reads: "BROOKLYN RAILROAD."

INT. TRAIN - DAY

Working professionals crowd the train car.
Some stand.

Among them is SALLY STANWICK, 25, pretty
in a simple cotton dress.  She turns
abruptly, sensing someone's stares.

A young man in a suit greets her with a
smug smile.
```

Now this is not brilliant writing, but it serves our purposes here. The first image is the train, establishing departure location and destination. The second image is of the people in the train car. The third paragraph describes a character and her action. And the fourth describes the actions of the second character.

Please note that I omit Sally's eye and hair color to keep casting options open. I omit the specifics of her clothes because they are irrelevant. I give her a simple cotton dress as a way to comment on her character—this is an uncomplicated young woman.

In a word, make sure your dialogue and narrative description are lean and move the story forward. Doing so will help your career move forward as well.

HEADINGS AND MASTER SCENES

QUESTION
I have sequences in which several scenes occur in different rooms of the same building. Right now the scene headings read something like this:

INT. BUILDING/JOE'S APARTMENT/LIVING ROOM

INT. BUILDING/CORRIDOR OUTSIDE JOE'S ROOM

INT. BUILDING/GARAGE

Some books say the above is proper form, but you seem to suggest otherwise in *The Screenwriter's Bible*.

ANSWER
What you have written above is fine, although you're missing two things.

1. The time. Does this scene take place in the day or night (for example, INT. BUILDING - DAY)? Remember the reader must be oriented to three things in a scene: Where the camera is (INT. or EXT.), location, and time (usually DAY or NIGHT).

2. Readability. Although your example is legal, it's difficult to read. That's why I suggest an alternative that I believe makes the script easier to read.

First set up a master scene, then cut to smaller locations contained within that master scene. In the example below, we begin with a master scene heading, then move to locations within that master scene location by using secondary headings.

```
INT. APARTMENT BUILDING - DAY

IN JOE'S APARTMENT

AT THE REFRIGERATOR

THE CORRIDOR OUTSIDE THE APARTMENT

IN THE GARAGE
```

All of these secondary locations can be found within the master location, the apartment building. Once we're out of the apartment building, establish a new master scene. The main thing is to make the script readable without losing the reader.

SET-UP EXPLANATION FOR QUESTIONS
I've been editing a sequence in a script of mine, and wondered just how I should go about designating scene headings in a dogfight; i.e., a battle between planes (or tanks, or spaceships), with cuts to inside individual vehicles and back to the battlefield itself. I'm talking about sequences like those in TOP GUN or STAR WARS (whose scripts I'd consult if I could find them).

[Let me interject here that there are many businesses that sell scripts. Just keep in mind when you buy a script that it is likely a *shooting script*, while you are writing a *spec script*, so avoid the camera directions and technical intrusions you'll see in the shooting script.]

Right now, things in my script look roughly like this:

```
EXT. SKY ABOVE THE MEDITERRANEAN - DAY

An enemy plane gets behind Johnny's
fighter.
```

```
INT. EAGLE TWO
```

Jimmy looks to his right at EAGLE ONE.

> JIMMY
> Look out, Johnny!

```
EXT. SKY
```

Eagle One dodges and weaves while the enemy fires at him.

> JIMMY (VO)
> He's on your tail!

```
INT. EAGLE ONE
```

Johnny pulls up on the stick.

> JOHNNY
> Thanks for the tip!

QUESTION 1
Would you treat the entire battle as one master scene?

ANSWER
Actually, what you have written above looks fine to me, at least in terms of formatting. On the other hand, you could treat the battle as a master scene with a master scene heading followed by several secondary headings. In that case, the sequence would look something like this:

```
EXT. SKY ABOVE THE MEDITERRANEAN - DAY

INSIDE EAGLE TWO

JUST ABOVE THE WATER
```

```
OUTSIDE ENEMY FIGHTER

INSIDE EAGLE ONE

OUTSIDE EAGLE TWO
```

The key is not so much to be technically correct, but to be clear and readable. As long as the reader can easily visualize what you are describing, then you'll be okay.

QUESTION 2
How would you indicate time during the battle? Would you put "SAME" after each scene heading?

ANSWER
You could if it is not otherwise obvious that these scenes all take place at the same time. In this case, I think the reader would naturally assume that we are in the *same* moment of time and that this is one battle and one main battle location.

QUESTION 3
Am I missing any other elements in making this rather complicated sequence comprehensible?

ANSWER
If you crosscut between two locations (back and forth), consider using the INTERCUT.

One important key in writing headings is to be clear and accurate, not clever or cute.

Questions for this section were submitted by Chris DelliCarpini.

GETTING DOWN TO BRASS BRADS

QUESTION
Although the script is three-hole punched, do I only use two brads? And what size brads do I use?

ANSWER
It is fashionable to leave the middle hole without a brad and only use two brads. I use ACCO No. 5 Brass Fasteners. They are 1 1/4" in length. I like ACCO because they are sturdier than the more flimsy brads I've seen elsewhere. ACCO pays me nothing to say this.

Some writers wonder why producers and agents prefer brass brads to more permanent forms of binding, such as a spiral binding. Many readers like to read loose pages. In addition, if a producer likes your script, he or she will rip out the two brass brads and photocopy it to show to others in the company (to solicit their opinions). If your script is permanently bound, it cannot be easily photocopied.

MUSIC AND SONG TITLES

QUESTION
While I do not score the screenplay by naming specific songs, may I write something like DRAMATIC MUSIC PLAYS? If the character turns on the radio, may I write, "Jason flips on the radio, which plays 'Do You Believe in Magic?' by the Lovin' Spoonful"?

ANSWER
You do not name a specific song title unless you control the rights to that song. No exceptions. When you list a specific

song title, the producer believes that only that song will make the story work (otherwise, why would you list it?), and if you don't have rights to the song, then the producer will have to secure them. You've just created a legal obstacle to selling your script.

Seldom do you indicate music in the script. Your job is to write a clear and compelling story. If you've established mood and subtext through your excellent writing, then the director and music composer will know when and where to insert the music, and what kind of music to compose.

If a character turns on a radio, then indicate music in a generic way. For example, "Jason flips on the radio, which plays an upbeat sixties tune." That's the safest course to follow.

CREDITS AND TITLES

QUESTION
Do I write ROLL CREDITS?

ANSWER
No. There is no need to. The director and producer will make that decision.

Often, when a writer indicates credits, he or she demonstrates his or her ignorance. How long should the credits roll? How do you make that judgment, for example, with opening credits? You would need to write CREDITS ROLL and then you'd have to indicate at some point END CREDITS. Don't mess with this stuff.

Just write the story in specific language so that the reader sees, hears, and feels. That's your job.

WHEN THE COMPUTER SPEAKS

QUESTION
I am writing a script which has a dialogue situation between two people via e-mail. Thus, from a computer user's POV, he types an answer to another person's e-mailed question. The answer then appears on the computer user's monitor and so on. Do I write this just as if they were actually speaking the words, or do I do something like this in narrative description: John sees the answer on the screen and responds, "Blah, blah, blah."

Or, if I write it as dialogue, should I preface this dialogue sequence with something like this? "The following conversation appears on John's monitor from his POV."

ANSWER
First of all, only words that are spoken appear as dialogue. That is what dialogue is. However, if a person repeats out loud what he/she reads on the monitor, then you could write what he/she actually says as dialogue.

Otherwise, you want to find a clear way that doesn't confuse the reader or slow down the read. Perhaps, something like this:

```
John faces his computer monitor, then
begins typing on the keyboard.

ON JOHN'S MONITOR

the words appear:

          "But Renee, they're tapping
          my phone conversations."

BACK TO JOHN
```

```
who studies Renee's response, then
chuckles.

ON  JOHN'S  MONITOR

Renee's response appears:

          "You're being silly, John."
```

This is just one of many ways to handle this (and please note that you should indent the words that are typed, just as if they *were* dialogue).

Avoid using POV or other such camera angles. The reason I like the above is because it's easy to read and absolutely clear what is happening. However, it does take a lot of space, so there might be a way to shorten it (perhaps omitting the phase "the words appear" and "Renee's response appears").

A CAST OF THOUSANDS

QUESTION
How would you refer to characters who are "cannon fodder"; i.e., the numerous anonymous characters who may have one line? At some point, the simple description fails; e.g., COMPUTER TECHNICIAN #27. Would you give them all names for the sake of simplicity, even though they'll never be called by their names?

ANSWER
It's hard to imagine a script with 27 technicians, all with speaking parts. To be honest, I've never seen that many anonymous characters in a script that was sold, optioned, or produced. That's because writers try to give the dialogue to the main characters.

As a general rule, you only give names to major and minor characters who are "important." Characters with only one or two lines *may* be given names, but usually *aren't* given names so that the reader knows not to focus on them. (You see, the reader feels that he/she must keep track of any characters who have names and speaking parts, especially early in the script.) So instead, refer to these unimportant characters in a way that makes them easy to visualize or distinguish: GRUFF TECH, SEXY TECH, SHY GEEK, and so on.

Let me summarize with another example. If you have six police officers speaking in a scene (POLICEMAN 1, POLICEMAN 2, and so on), my first reaction is to recommend that you reduce the number of speaking police officers to one or two. If any of these six officers is an important character, try to give him/her most of the lines. If these officers are not important (have no lines, or have just one line, or only appear in one or two scenes), I would distinguish them in some visual way: MACHO COP, TOOTH PICK, CHUBBY COP, etc. This makes them easier to visualize and signals to the reader that they are not particularly important.

BEING FANCY IS CHANCY

QUESTION
Should I include special effects sketches or story boards with my script?

ANSWER
No. The reader wants a script that tells a story. Do not include drawings, sketches, story boards, fancy title pages, special binding, special fonts, bold typeface, italic typeface, etc. Just present a well-written, emotionally satisfying story that we can visualize, written in correct spec format.

SINGING THE BLUES

QUESTION
What is the industry-accepted format for writing song lyrics into a character's dialogue? My script concerns a song writer, and I'm uncertain as to what formatting technique I use to write her song numbers into the script. I can't find the answer anywhere.

ANSWER
The reason you don't see much information on this "formatting technique" is because it is not generally used in spec scripts.

It sounds like your character writes songs and so the songs are an important part of the story. But in so doing, you're asking the eventual producer to either accept the music you have already written or to find someone to write music to your lyrics. So not only does the producer have to love your story, he or she has to love the lyrics and the music as well.

Soundtrack movies are almost always developed at a production company or studio. The rights to the music are secured during or before the development process. Musicals are usually plays before they are movies; in such cases, the rights to the original play are purchased before the screenplay is written. Seldom are musicals and music-based movies purchased as spec scripts.

If the songs you want to include in your story are written by existing artists, then you shouldn't write in their lyrics unless you own or control the rights to their songs, nor should you mention specific songs in your spec script.

These are all reasons it is generally a good idea to avoid music altogether in a spec script and just tell a good story. Coincidentally, I recently wrote a script about a rock star. There are obvious places for music in my script, but I never mention specific songs, nor do I write out any lyrics. That can be done later, after the script is sold.

Now that I've laid all the negatives down, let me say that it is possible that a producer will love your script, music, and lyrics just the way they are. In such a case, the music may help cinch the deal. It only takes one person to love your story.

Finally, here's the answer to your question. When you write the lyrics of a song, you write them as dialogue since they are sung by a character. You can write them in stanza form just like a poem, or you can use slashes as follows:

```
                    DAN
       The higher you climb/the more
       that you see/The more that you
       see/the less that you know/The
       less that you know/the more
       that you yearn/The more that
       you yearn/the higher you climb.
```

That's one of my favorites from Dan Fogelberg (*High Country Snows* © 1985 CBS Inc.).

AND THE REST IS HISTORY

QUESTION
I am presently working on a screenplay about the local history. How can I get a quick copyright on my idea just in case someone else stumbles on to what I am writing about?

ANSWER
History cannot be copyrighted, and ideas cannot be copyrighted.

You cannot protect your ideas, premises, titles, plot lines, etc. You can only protect your original expression of an idea--your screenplay.

History is in the public domain, meaning that it belongs to everyone. However, you cannot base your screenplay on an historical book without getting the rights to that book.

Finally, if the local history you refer to is recent and not well-known, you may need to get the rights to the story from the participants. This question and all legal questions should be addressed to a competent entertainment attorney.

MOVIE CLIPS

QUESTION
How do I write out my opening scene if I'm using a clip from another movie?

ANSWER
You cannot use a clip from another movie unless you control the rights to that movie. Do not open your screenplay with a scene from an existing movie. Do not base your screenplay on any work that you do not control the rights to. Do not write the sequel to SNOW WHITE unless you control the rights to SNOW WHITE. Just write an original screenplay.

Obviously, you may briefly refer to other movies in a character's dialogue if doing so moves the story forward or adds to character. For example, in SLEEPLESS IN SEATTLE, there are references to THE DIRTY DOZEN and AN AFFAIR TO REMEMBER. But don't write, "He turned on the TV and the sinking scene from TITANIC was showing." Doing that will give you a sinking feeling when your script is rejected.

VERBS, ADJECTIVES, AND WISDOM

QUESTION
Dr. Format, you often talk about using specific verbs to describe actions without adverbs, and using specific nouns without using adjectives. Are you saying that adjectives and adverbs should be avoided whenever possible?

ANSWER
No, I'm saying that you won't need to use nearly as many adjectives and adverbs if you use specific, concrete nouns and verbs.   For example, here's a sentence with an adverb and adjective in it: *He ran quickly to the little house.* Here is the same sentence, only this time using a concrete verb and a concrete noun: *He raced to the cottage.* Because I am using concrete language, I do not need the adverb and adjective.

However, even when you use concrete nouns and verbs, you still may see a need for concrete adjectives and adverbs.   In the following sentence, I add a couple of adjectives for visual clarification: *He raced to the red brick bungalow.* Thus, my real point is this: Use concrete, visual language in your narrative description.

I have an interesting quote from the late, great Paddy Cheyvsky (*Marty, Network*), who said, "I have two rules. First, cut out all the wisdom; then, cut out all the adjectives." I don't think he means he actually goes through the script and omits every adjective; I believe he is referring to lean, concrete language. The "cutting out all the wisdom" alludes to the tendency for some scripts to become preachy, or overstate their theme, or use pretentious, unnatural dialogue.

MUTE DIALOGUE

QUESTION
How do you write dialogue for a character that is mute?

ANSWER
That depends on how that "dialogue" is communicated to the audience.

First of all, *signing* is not dialogue since words are not actually spoken. Of course, general audiences are not familiar with signing, so usually (in a film script) the mute person's meaning is communicated to the audience either verbally or through subtitles. If the mute person speaks as he/she signs, then simply write the words he/she says as dialogue:

```
                    MUTE PERSON
                 (while signing)
          Did you understand what I said?
```

If the mute person is a major character, then indicate once in the narrative description that the mute person signs whenever he/she talks; that way, you won't need to include a parenthetical for each block of dialogue.

If the dialogue is written in subtitles across the screen, then write out the dialogue as in the example above, except write the parenthetical as follows: "while signing; in subtitles." An alternative method is to indicate in narrative description that the mute person signs and that the dialogue appears in subtitles.

As always in spec writing, your goal is to be as clear and unobtrusive as you can.

EFFECTS THAT ARE SPECIAL

QUESTION
I have several scenes in my script that call for the use of special effects. It's not an "event" film, but a character piece that utilizes special effects for dramatic understanding.

My question is, how do you indicate the transition to the special effect? For example, do I write it as follows?

```
Steve takes a puff from the pipe.

FX. - WE SEE STEVE LEVITATE SLOWLY ABOVE
THE FLOOR, STILL IN HIS SQUATTED POSITION.

STEVE'S POV - We then SEE the muted COLORS
of the room begin to BRIGHTEN intensely.
```

Or do I simply write it as a normal scene description?

ANSWER
What you have written above is correct for a shooting script. In a spec script, avoid using technical language. When the script is converted into a shooting script, all the technical language will be added. Here's one way to revise this for a spec script.

```
Steve, sitting cross-legged on the floor,
takes a puff from the pipe. Slowly he
levitates.

He sees the muted colors of the room
brighten intensely.
```

That's it. You might consider breaking to a new paragraph for "Slowly he levitates" to make that special effect stand out more, but no special language is required. Isn't that special?

I SPY

QUESTION
I want to write a movie scene where someone is under surveillance, but he doesn't know it. As we see him going up stairs into a public building, we hear (off screen) the sound of a 35 mm camera's shutter clicking. I would be interested in knowing how to write this in the proper format.

ANSWER
Is there something you're not telling me? This seems too straight forward.

```
EXT. PUBLIC BUILDING - DAY

James Connors hurries up the cement
stairs.

An unseen person clicks the shutter of a
35 mm camera.  Clicks again.  And again as
James rushes into the building.
```

Of course, there are many ways to stage this scene and write the narrative. If you were writing a shooting script, you could use a POV (point-of-view) shot. If you feel so compelled, you could CAP the "clicks," since they are important sounds.

A SUPER JOB

QUESTION
Although I understand the use of SUPERs now, I'm unclear about how a spec script indicates that words are to appear on the screen...the way films will show a sentence to set background history (or historical data) before the first scene. This would be

like say, "California 1998" superimposed on the screen.

ANSWER
That's precisely what SUPER stands for—superimposition. When you write

```
SUPER: "California, 1998"
```

you are indicating that the words being quoted are to be superimposed over the image on the screen.

FOLLOW-UP QUESTION
What if it's more than one sentence? Also: If it appears at the beginning of the movie, does the writer simply type these sentences or legends out at the top of the script after "FADE IN:"?

ANSWER
First present an image, and then the superimposition. Here's an example that utilizes a longer "legend."

```
EXT. LOS ANGELES - DAY

The city sparkles in the sunlight.

SUPER:  "Los Angeles, December 31, 1999.
It's an hour before midnight, an hour
before millions of computers pass into
oblivion...."
```

If you want to SUPER paragraphs, you may wish to consider using a SCROLL or ROLL-UP as in all of the STAR WARS episodes.

TREATMENT FORMAT

QUESTION
Is the normal 3-4 page selling treatment double-spaced?

ANSWER
Yes. Remember that a treatment is a written pitch—a marketing piece—and should include the character and his/her problem, the main turning points, and the emotional highlights. It's written in narrative form with no or little dialogue.

LOST IN THE BOOKSTORE

QUESTION
I have a short scene in a bookstore. In the scene, a character goes into a restroom. Do I use a secondary heading? And how do I take the reader back into the bookstore—do I use the master scene heading again?

ANSWER
Just make the scene as clear as possible. First, establish the master scene with a master scene heading (slug line), and then use secondary headings to direct our eyes. Here's a possible list of headings in your scene, beginning with the master scene heading:

```
INT. BOOKSTORE - DAY

IN THE BATHROOM

BACK IN THE BOOKSTORE
```

...And so on, until you start a new master scene.

QUOTES WITHIN DIALOGUE

QUESTION
Is it legal to use a quotation from Nietzsche in dialogue if the character speaking says, "Nietzsche says..."?

ANSWER
I am not qualified to give legal advice and nothing I write should be construed as such.

With that disclaimer out of the way, I can answer your question: Of course. If it's just a line or two, you can quote anyone, just as you can in a book. In one of my comedies, my hero, a philosopher, has the worst day of his life. The punch line at the end of the scene goes like this.

```
                    PHILBERT
         So Kafka was right.   Man is
         helpless to control his fate.
```

MINI-FLASHBACKS AND VOICE OVERS

QUESTION
How do you handle a quick memory hit? Let's say a man is telling a story to a friend about a friend getting killed by a train 30 years ago. Do I just write the image of a train killing David? [Apparently, David is the questioner's character who is killed; either that, or it's a secret message to me.] Do I need any caption such as a memory hit or quick flash?

ANSWER
A memory hit? I don't think that term has hit the mainstream lexicon yet.

The standard response to questions of this type is this: Write what we see. What does the audience see? If you actually show the train, then that is a flashback and you will want to indicate it as a flashback. You must label it as such so that we clearly understand that it is a flashback.

If your character (let's call him Zep) speaks while we see the flashback, then use the voice over (VO) device. .

```
FLASHBACK - TRAIN TRACKS

David sees a train coming.  In a surreal
game of chicken, he places himself on the
tracks.

                    ZEP (VO)
          David always flirted with
          disaster...

With the train nearly upon him, David
tries to leap from the tracks, but his
shirt catches on a rail tie.

He glances up at the unforgiving mass of
steel.

                    ZEP (VO)
          ...Then one day, disaster
          responded.

The wheels of the train slice through his
body.
```

This is not great screenwriting, but we can learn three lessons from it.

1. Notice that I avoided repeating in dialogue what we already see visually. Whenever you use a voice over in situations like

this, let that voice over dialogue add something that the visual does not already tell us. Don't just describe in your dialogue the action that you describe in your narrative.

2. Do not write something as general as "The train ran over him." Present us with concrete, visual images that we can respond to emotionally or intellectually.

3. Start a new paragraph when you switch to a new visual image. Generally, a paragraph of narrative description should present one visual image or one beat of action. (I hasten to add that that is a very general guideline.)

For more on flashback formatting, go on to the next question about dream sequences.

DREAM SEQUENCES

QUESTION
I'm writing a dream or a nightmare sequence as a reoccurring motif, but how do I inform the reader that it is a dream and not something else? Do I have to say something in the scene slug line like EXT. DREAM SEQUENCE, or do I just describe it in the action description? If so, what do I write? Is there a right or wrong way to do this?

ANSWER
As implied in my previous answer about flashbacks, you should clearly label anything that is not normal narrative action. The exception comes when you want to hide that fact from the audience. In the situation you describe, I suspect that you want the reader to know that what he/she sees is a dream or dream sequence. (Incidentally, nightmares are dreams.) So let's approach your question from that angle.

First of all, you cannot write EXT. DREAM SEQUENCE because a dream sequence is not a location.

Second, make sure your heading (or slug line) is correctly labeled.

If the dream takes place in a single scene, just write:

EXT. CITY STREET - NIGHT - DREAM

or

EXT. CITY STREET - NIGHT (DREAM)

or

DREAM - A DIMLY LIT STREET

However, if this is a dream sequence that takes place over two scenes or more, write:

DREAM SEQUENCE

EXT. CITY STREET - NIGHT

Then write out the scenes until the dream ends, and then write:

END OF DREAM SEQUENCE

This same formatting style is used for flashbacks.

I hope these tips help you make your dreams come true.

A BLOCKBUSTER QUERY

QUESTION
I have just finished a script that could be the next blockbuster movie. Also, I have two other blockbuster scripts written. I'm thinking of querying all these scripts at the same time, indicating that all of them are blockbusters. What do you think?

ANSWER
The agent probably won't believe you. That's because many developing screenwriters make the same claim and then don't deliver. In fact, I've evaluated a number of "blockbusters" myself.

Additionally, your best strategy in a query is to *show* rather than *tell*. In other words, don't tell the agent you have three blockbusters, pitch your biggest blockbuster in such a way that the agent can see that you have written a blockbuster. You may mention in your letter that you have two other scripts written.

Good luck and keep writing.

WORKING WITH DRILL INSTRUCTORS

QUESTION
Dr. Format, you have said to avoid exclamation points. I'm writing a spec script set in the military. There are scenes where drill instructors are barking orders at grunts. It seems to me that the script would lose its punch during scenes like that.

ANSWER
My advice is to *avoid* exclamation points, not eliminate them entirely. There are two main reasons to avoid them. First, you

don't want your dialogue looking like a garage sale ad. Second, you don't want to tell actors how to say their lines unless necessary. There is a line in the screenplay PLAY MISTY FOR ME that is followed by multiple exclamation points. However, in the movie, the actress says that line ever so softly, and it has a decidedly eerie and threatening effect.

Keep the next point in mind as well: If the context of the dialogue indicates that the actor would shout, then you don't need exclamation points because it's already obvious that he/she would shout. In your case, the military context is probably clear enough. However, if you feel you are losing the "punch" of the scene, go ahead with the exclamation points, but consider using them only in moments where it's not otherwise obvious that the drill sergeant would be shouting.

Finally, using exclamation points or not using them is not going to make or break your script, unless your script starts looking like a want ad.

WORKING WITH PSYCHICS

QUESTION
Let's say a character is a psychic and he's giving another character an account of what he sees. If I'm trying to show the "account" visually with the character speaking, how do I write it?

ANSWER
Simply describe what we see on the screen. Write it like a regular scene with VOICE OVER (V.O.) dialogue. You will use VOICE OVER because the character speaking is not in the scene.

```
                    PSYCHIC (V.O.)
          You are coming into some money.
```

```
A homeless man holds out his hand and
receives a dollar from a passer-by.
```

WORKING WITH RABBIS

QUESTION
I am writing a funeral scene. The officiating rabbi is talking to the mourners about the deceased. One of the characters notices something happening on the cemetery road. I want to write what the character sees, but at the same time, hear what the officiating rabbi is saying. How do I do this?

ANSWER
What will the eventual movie audience see and hear? In this case, they will see what is happening on the cemetery road while they hear the words of the rabbi nearby. The rabbi is in the scene, but not on screen, so his dialogue will be OFF SCREEN (O.S.), as follows.

```
Sharon looks up the

CEMETERY ROAD

where three teenagers break into her car.

                    RABBI (O.S.)
          The Lord giveth and the Lord
          taketh away.
```

WORKING WITH EMPATHS

QUESTION
Due to the science fiction nature of my script, some of my characters are empaths or telepaths. How does one technically

say that the characters speak "empathically"? Do I write "empathically" as a parenthetical? Here's my example.

```
                    EMPATH
                (empathically)
        I am reading you, Chester.
```

ANSWER
Only spoken words can be written as dialogue. Dialogue is spoken speech. So you must find some other way. In STAR TREK, I have seen the empath simply state what she is *sensing* or *reading*. Thus, the audience knows what she is picking up.

Here is a question for *you*: If there is an actual telepathic communication, how will the audience know what is being communicated? In other words, what does the audience see and hear in the movie theater? Whatever it is, that is what you must describe in your screenplay. If the audience hears words (without anyone's lips moving), then clearly describe that and use a VOICE OVER for the words, although it's probably too hokey to use in a dramatic or serious work.

THE STORY'S THE THING

QUESTION
I have a scene in a large control room. The room is full of busy technicians conversing, including two main characters. Should I write the lines of everyone who speaks, including all of the background chatter and noise? It seems like cop-out not including all the background chatter.

ANSWER
Unless the chatter is important to the essential story, why include it at all? Focus on the story.

QUESTION
I want to write a story about my wife who passed away. I want to show others what a caring person she was. I want to include a scene of her referring to her childhood when she wondered what she was going to be when she grew up. We won't see her talking; instead, we will see her as a child and also as what she wanted to become. How do I handle that?

ANSWER
There are two ways to handle this: 1) You present the visuals just as they will appear on the silver screen. Your wife's dialogue would be handled as a voice over. 2) If you decide to show her speaking, then you will cut to flashforwards (if what see is in the future) or flashbacks (if what we see is in the past). A third choice would be to combine these two styles--sometimes we see her talking and sometimes she narrates (voice over).

A word of caution: This scene you refer to along with the screenplay will be a wonderful memory for you, but how will you make that memory come alive for an audience who never knew your wife and who have no emotional feeling for her when they walk into the theater?

Keep in mind that real life doesn't often translate naturally to dramatic structure. A true story almost always has to be restructured and changed, with time condensed and characters combined and even altered. And, of course, there must be a clear, compelling story with a beginning, middle, and end.

PHYSIOLOGY 101

QUESTION
When you are creating your characters for your script, do you have to determine all of the physiology? If I were to determine

that, then it would be hard for the director to find an actor for the role.

ANSWER
The physiology of your characters is seldom important to the screenplay for the reason you stated, but it should be important to you. You need to be able to visualize your character and have a definite "person" in mind when you write.

GOOD WILL TO ALL

QUESTION
Conventional wisdom suggests that there must be a clear goal and an antagonist, but I don't buy it. I've seen many movies where there appears to be neither a concrete goal nor an antagonist. Take GOOD WILL HUNTING. The movie seems completely driven by Will's need to love himself before he can be close to others. And the opposition is his own character flaws. Where's the goal?

ANSWER
That is a great question. In character-driven stories, the need always supersedes the goal. There are many movies where the goal is very thin or practically non-existent. (In STAND BY ME, the goal is to find the body.) In the case of GOODWILL HUNTING, notice the individual sequences. In those, you will see that Will often has an intention or desire; for example, he wants to put the arrogant college dude in his place and get Minnie Driver's phone number. That scene is driven by a goal that reveals something of his character.

Also, notice that there are at least two opposition characters. Robin Williams--and to a lesser degree, Minnie Drive--oppose his goal/desire/intention to remain undiscovered and closed off from others and his own goodness. In addition, Robin Williams is opposed by a colleague. And then, in individual scenes, you have the arrogant college dude, the university professor, and Will's best friend as opposition characters. So everyone has an intention, desire, or goal of some sort throughout the story, providing plenty of conflict. But at the core of the story is Will's need.

Your need (and goal) is to write a great story and gain the good will of an agent or producer.

WATCH YOUR FRENCH

QUESTION
In the screenplay I'm working on, I have a scene where the guests of a duchess are entertained by a tableaux vivant. How do I format the tableaux?

ANSWER
The first rule of formatting is to describe what we see. So what do we see in this tableaux? And where does it take place? Every scene has a location. The location is identified in the heading (slug line). I'm going to assume that we see this on a stage and that the duchess and her guests are in the audience.

```
INT. THEATER - NIGHT

The duchess and her guests gather in the
few luxury chairs that face a stage.

ON THE STAGE

the curtain rises to a tableaux vivant.
```

Now describe what the movie audience sees. What happens?

Occasionally, we may cut to the duchess who approves or disapproves with an applause or a gesture. This is essentially a play within a play. Just write what we see.

STUCK IN A MOVIE THEATER

QUESTION
I am trying to write a screenplay for which several scenes take place inside a movie theater. The action and dialogue that occur on the screen are integral to the story, but I'm not sure how to write the on-screen action to distinguish it from the action in the theater itself.

ANSWER
It sounds like you are going to have to cross-cut between the screen (ON THE SCREEN) and in the theater (IN THE THEATER).

```
ON THE SCREEN

The Baywatch Kid draws his pistol.   Fires
twice.

IN THE THEATER

A disturbed young man stands and fires
back at the Baywatch Kid, only with real
bullets.
```

In addition, my responses to the tableaux vivant question above and the TV question on the next page will help you with this question because the three situations are related.

TELEVISION TALK

QUESTION
I'm writing a scene where people are watching a newscast on the television. We see the reporter on TV. How do I write what the reporter says?

In the next scene, we go to the White House where the reporter is reporting and we hear a continuation of his report.

ANSWER
In the first scene, do we see the reporter on TV or do we just hear him? If we just hear him, then it is VOICE OVER dialogue.

```
                    TV REPORTER (VO)
          I am standing in front of the
          White House...
```

If we see the reporter on TV as he speaks, then remove the VOICE OVER (VO).

Next, cut to the White House.

```
EXT. WHITE HOUSE - CONTINUOUS

The TV reporter continues.  A huge crowd
observes.

                    TV REPORTER
          ...And, as you can see, it has
          been painted blue.
```

Incidentally, I used the ellipsis to show continuity in dialogue.

NO ONE IS COUNTING

QUESTION
How many lines per page are there in a screenplay?

ANSWER
Believe me, no one is counting. And if any one is, that person could probably use some therapy. Just do your margins correctly and you'll be in fine shape: 1 1/2 inches on the left, 1 inch on the right (you can stretch this to 1/2 inch if need be), and 1 inch on the top and bottom.

AS EASY AS CLASSICAL GREEK

QUESTION
My character is at a point of making a decision and will take an action either one way or the other. She recalls an event from the past, back to her, another event from the past, back to her, another event from the past, back to her, etc. Is this a series of shots? a montage? a flashback? Each event recalled is just a moment—it is clearly in her mind with the focus always on her.

I actually studied Classical Greek and it was easier than film formatting.

ANSWER
There are several ways to handle this, whether in Greek or in English. Here are two.

1. Simply cut back and forth, from the present scene to a flashback, and so on. Each cut to the past is a flashback, regardless of how short that flashback is, but the focus will be on the decision. This style is similar to what M. Night Shyamalan

did at the end of *The Sixth Sense* when Bruce Willis comes to his realization.

2. You could label the whole thing...

```
MONTAGE - SUSAN'S DECISION
```

...and then simply describe each shot that we see. Every other shot will be a flashback.

In terms of content, I worry about this sequence just a little. What is this woman (we're calling her Susan) doing in the present as she moves forward to make her decision? I'm hoping she's physically moving towards some action and not in some kind of internal dialogue or chatting with a friend. Give the scene some movement and visual elements.

CHEATERS NEVER PROSPER

QUESTION
Can you cheat on the spacing between the lines to add lines to a page?

ANSWER
Do not alter the spacing so that you can cram another line or two onto the page. Any professional reader will immediately recognize your deception, and he/she won't be happy about it.

FOR WHOM THE BELL TOLLS

QUESTION
Which should be capitalized? "The BELL rang" or "The bell RANG"?

ANSWER
These days, neither. Just write, "The bell rang." If you wish, you may capitalize important sounds that you want to emphasize, in which case, it would be "The bell RANG."

THE WGA NOTICE

QUESTION
I find conflicting opinions as to whether or not it is proper to include a WGA notice and number on the title page of a script.

ANSWER
I recommend that you type "Registered WGAw (or WGAe) No._____" in the lower, left-hand corner of the title page. In my mind, I am serving notice that I have registered my script. Make sure that you register your script with the WGA before you send it out to anyone.

ACTION STACKING

QUESTION
Lately I've been hearing about a popular way to write action called *action stacking*. I was wondering if you could give me an example of what this looks like. I don't think I have read a screenplay that shows this type of format.

ANSWER
Action stacking is a style of writing that literally stacks a series of short actions in a scene using single spacing. Here's an example.

```
EXT. BALLPARK - DAY

Duke sneers at the catcher.
Taps the bat twice on his cleats.
```

```
Spits a brown wad on home plate.
Allows himself a self-satisfied grin.
```

Notice that these are short sentences stacked one on top of the other; thus, *action stacking*. See my comments on pages 71-72.

WRITING ACTION

QUESTION
On one hand, you say to dramatize important actions, while on the other hand, you say to "write lean." Can you provide an example of something that is both sparse and dramatic?

ACTION
I have seen many writers translate the word "lean" into "vague" or "no details." Actually, the opposite is true. "Writing lean" is choosing your details carefully and using specific, concrete words (especially verbs and nouns) to describe them. It's providing the reader with only what's necessary to *see* and *understand clearly* what's happening in the scene.

I would like to provide you with a "spec script" version of a brief excerpt from MISERY (© 1990 Castle Rock Entertainment, excerpted from *The Hollywood Scriptwriter*) by William Goldman. Annie is about to chop off Paul's foot with an axe.

```
PAUL

shrieks as there is a terrible thudding
sound -- and then his body jackknifes. He
is beyond agony as blood splashes over his
neck, his face, and

ANNIE

her face splashed with blood and
```

THE SHEET

turning red and

ANNIE

eyes dull, getting into position again.

> ANNIE
> Once more and we're all done.

PAUL

as again there is the thudding sound, and he's incoherent. Animal sounds come from him as

ANNIE

takes a match, lights the propane torch with the match, and there's a sound as the yellow flame appears.

> ANNIE
> No time to suture, got to cauterize.

She brings the flame closer. Paul shrieks even louder.

> ANNIE
> God, I love you....

Whew! Some novice writers would simply write:

She chops off his foot. He screams madly. She lights the torch and cauterizes the wound.

And there are others who might describe every detail over four pages. That, of course, would be overdoing it, or *overwriting*.

I'd like to make one last comment about that last line of dialogue. Try to end your scenes with something that is strong, or something that moves us into the next scene or a future scene. In the above scene, we have a very strong punch line in Annie's declaration of "love."

WHAT'S IN A NAME?

QUESTION
If a character has a nickname throughout the movie (i.e., killer), but his real name is Bob Franklin, do I call him Killer or Franklin or Bob where his name appears in the dialogue block [referring to the *character cue* or *character caption* in the dialogue block]?

ANSWER
It's your choice. Whichever you choose, it should be consistent throughout the entire script. When I say consistent, I mean a *consistent character cue*. In other words, whenever this character speaks, the character name you use (let's choose Franklin) should always be the same.

```
                FRANKLIN
      Be outa town by sunset or
      you're dead meat.
```

However, you can call him anything you want to in the narrative description and dialogue speeches. Just be consistent in the character cue.

As a very general rule, by the way, call good guys by their first name and bad guys by their last name in the character cue.

FORMATTING QUERY LETTERS

QUESTION
I know that you recommend 12-point Courier (or New Courier) for screenplays, but what about query letters? Is Times New Roman or Arial cool, or should I stick to Courier? Any other formatting rules I should know? Also, what should be the word count for a query letter?

ANSWER
You have more latitude in a query letter, but keep in mind that your query letter should be formatted like a business letter, although the actual content will reveal you as a superb, creative writer. Fancy graphics are not necessary; after all, you are selling yourself as a writer, not as a graphic artist. Using your own letterhead is fine.

You may use Times New Roman or Arial, but don't use a script typeface or any typeface that might, in any way, be difficult to read. I favor a 12-point font. I also recommend standard block format, which means everything is brought to the left margin. Double space between paragraphs and don't indent. (Other business letter formats are fine.)

As to word count, I don't count words. I shoot for three "brief" paragraphs. However, the letter needs to be long enough to convince the reader to call you, but short enough to lure someone into reading it. Big blocks of black ink won't do that.

HOW HIGH IS HIGH?

QUESTION
Does the notion of "high concept" apply to family movies as

well? When I think of *Otis and Milo* and *Homeward Bound*, I see similar concepts of animals trying to get home. If these films were still in the scripting stage, I wouldn't think they were high concept. Do you think they are?

ANSWER
Both of these movies have a concept--in other words, they can be easily conceptualized. Whether that concept is "high" or not is in the mind of the producer. One person might say "yes" for his or her particular market, while another may say "no" for his or her market.

The point is you need to be able to conceptualize your story. What is the concept? What is the story in 25 words or less? What is it about your story that will make your reader say "Now that's a movie"? A particularly strong rendition of the concept is called "high concept" because it makes the reader/listener feel "high"--"Ah, this is a movie I can sell to my market."

LOG LINES

QUESTION
What makes a good log line?

ANSWER
A book could be written on this, and the above explanation on "high concept" should be of some value to you. Here's a couple of ideas. A good logline is about a character with a problem that grabs the reader and says, "I am a movie."

A good logline is just that--one line, one sentence. A good logline can be a premise question (What if the president were kidnapped?) or a statement around a big event (When a child psychiatrist is shot by a patient, he redeems himself by helping a child who sees ghosts overcome his fear of them).

In virtually all cases, a logline cannot sell a script, but a good logline can position the movie in the reader's mind and make him or her want to read more.

SAY IT IN ENGLISH

QUESTION
Is "sotto voce" or simply "sotto" still used in parentheticals these days?

ANSWER
There's no need to use Latin unless you are a priest or a music composer.

Besides, you want to avoid soliloquies in spec scripts these days. If you absolutely must have a character say something to himself that the other characters do not hear, just use the term "aside" or "to self."

AN UN*BEAT*ING STRATEGY

QUESTION
What thoughts do you have on the use of the term "beat" in dialogue? According to Denny Martin Flinn, we should not use the term. He says to write "pause" or to detail the intended beat with a specific action.

ANSWER
I am in with Flinn. The term "beat" is a theatrical term and, although you see it in many shooting scripts and in Joe Ezsterhaus spec scripts, you can certainly find something more exciting to write than "beat." After all, you *are* a creative writer. Which of the following three examples creates more interest?

```
                    JANE
        Ed Darling, I want you to
        know...
                (beat)
        ...how much I love you.


                    JANE
        Ed Darling, I want you to
        know...
                (eyes mist up)
        ...how much I love you.


                    JANE
        Ed Darling, I want you to
        know...
                (suddenly sneezing
                all over Ed)
        ...how much I love you.
```

None of the three examples will win any prizes, but certainly the first is the boring one. The second is dramatic. The third is funny (or disgusting). Here is the point. The word "beat" is the most colorless, lifeless term you can use to indicate a pause. Instead, use specific words that add to the story or help characterize your character.

LATE ARRIVAL

QUESTION
If I were to introduce a character first through off-screen dialogue, what would I call him/her? Would you still use his/her name, even though he/she has not yet been introduced to the reader?

ANSWER
Try to introduce the character before he or she speaks.

If you can't do that, then use the cue FEMALE VOICE (assuming the character is a woman); and then, once we see her and you introduce her, start using her name as your character cue. Here's a quick example.

```
             FEMALE VOICE
        I want to tell you....
```

Ed parts the curtain and sees JANE, a twenty-something bombshell with hair tumbling everywhere.

```
             JANE
        ...how much I love you.
```

INSERTING THE GUN

QUESTION
How many INSERTS are allowed in a spec script?

ANSWER
Limit your use of the INSERT. In many cases, you may not need to use it at all. For example, if you want to emphasize the fact that there is a gun lying on the coffee table, simply write:

```
A gun lies on the coffee table.
```

THE WRITER AS DIRECTOR

QUESTION
We know that long before a script becomes a movie it is first a reading experience, and that we should avoid camera directions because that's the director's job. But there is a definite feel I wish to communicate in my first page. Here it is.

```
EXT. HIGHWAY 27 - DAY - AERIAL VIEW

WE SEE the lush Florida countryside until
we FIND our subject, a dark blue van.

SLOW ZOOM IN ON VAN

VIEW ON VAN - MOVING

Two characters shout at each other while
the CAMERA MOVES beside the van until we
see the child/protagonist looking out the
window at us.

INT. VAN - BUSTER, CAROL AND ABBIE

Everyone is quiet.
```

ANSWER
I would not call the above a riveting "reading experience."

Notice in the above example that the focus is on *how* the story is told, not on the story itself. What is going on in the car? We don't know. Who are the two characters? Why is the child looking out the window? What is his or her facial expression? Is the child a boy or a girl? We don't know because you are too involved *directing* your movie.

How can you improve this without sacrificing much in terms of the "feel" that you want to communicate? The revision that follows is not a masterpiece, but I hope you find it a better read than the original.

```
EXT. FLORIDA - DAY

From the Atlantic shore, the lush
countryside extends for miles westward.
Below, a black two-lane highway meanders
```

```
through the Spring growth.  A blue van
scoots down the highway.

EXT. VAN - SAME

The van rumbles along.  Inside, two
twenty-something parents, BUSTER and CAROL
shout at each other, although their words
cannot be heard.

Buster shoots an angry look to the back
where ABBIE, age 6, leans away from him
and stares out the window at the beautiful
trees and shrubs whizzing by.

AT THE WINDOW

The child is motionless, sad, trapped.
One little hand presses against the glass.

INT. VAN - SAME

The parents are silent now -- gathering
steam before their next eruption.
```

In the revision, I have *suggested* almost everything you wanted, but my focus is on the story and the characters, not on fancy-dancy ways to tell the story.

In addition, I also *imply* a POV shot of the child staring at the trees and shrubs. If desired, I could even describe the reflection of trees on the window glass (without using technical terms).

I also direct the camera (without using a camera direction) to a CLOSE UP of the child at the window. And I do that for a story reason. I want the reader to know that the child is the most important character in the scene, and that maybe she is the central character or protagonist; and I want the reader (and the movie audience) to emotionally identify with the child's situation.

I end the scene with a promise of things to come. I am trying to create some interest in what happens next while revealing the emotions of the parents.

In summary, my advice is to focus on story and character; and, while you are at it, use clear, specific language.

FADE OUT

QUESTION
After fading to black at the end of my screenplay, I want to do a succession of fade in/fade out captions listing the eventual fates of certain of the characters. How would I format this?

ANSWER
Just as you have described it.

                                        FADE OUT

FADE IN OVER BLACK SCREEN:

        "SLICK WILLY LATER WENT ON
        TO BECOME PRESIDENT OF THE
        UNITED STATES."

                                        FADE OUT

And so on.

MAKING SCENES

QUESTION
I am not clear on the use of DAY. It seems redundant to keep writing DAY in scene after scene that takes place within a single sequence. For example, if I am outside a warehouse and then move inside the warehouse, do I have to use DAY in both cases, as follows?

```
EXT. WAREHOUSE - DAY

INT. WAREHOUSE - DAY
```

ANSWER
First, let's discuss the fundamentals, then apply them.

Every *master scene* consists of three elements: 1) camera placement (EXT or INT), 2) location, and 3) time (usually DAY or NIGHT). Technically, when any one of the three elements changes, the scene changes. That's why *master scene headings* have three parts, one for each of the three elements that comprise a scene.

So when you move the camera inside the warehouse, you create a new scene that requires a new scene heading (slug line). That means that the two master scene headings above are correct.

If you feel that the repetition of DAY is redundant, you can apply certain alternatives as long as the three elements of the scene are clear to the reader.

If one scene follows the other scene in one continuous line of action without any jumps in time, you can write CONTINUOUS or SAME. Here's an example.

```
EXT. WAREHOUSE - DAY
```

Jake unlocks the warehouse door and pushes
the door open.

```
INT. WAREHOUSE - CONTINUOUS
```

Jake steps into the warehouse.

If that exterior scene is only there to establish Jake's presence and introduce the scene inside the warehouse, then you can use this alternative.

```
EXT./INT. WAREHOUSE - CONTINUOUS
```

Jake unlocks the warehouse door and steps
in.

That device is often used in car scene conversations. It gives the director the choice to place the camera inside the car or outside the car or both.

Occasionally, you can get away with omitting DAY, as follows.

```
EXT. WAREHOUSE - DAY
```

Jake unlocks the warehouse door and pushes
the door open.

```
INT. WAREHOUSE
```

Jake steps into the warehouse.

Only do that when the time (DAY or NIGHT) is absolutely clear to the reader, as in the example above. Sometimes writers get fancy or clever in their headings, only to confuse the reader. Clarity is one of the prime keys to great spec writing.

MASTERING SCENES

QUESTION
I've noticed that some screenplays use the complete slug line INT. BEDROOM - NIGHT [with all three scene elements included] while others use IN THE BEDROOM. Which is correct, or is it writer's choice?

ANSWER
Please note my use of the term *master scene heading* in my previous answer. A master scene heading is a heading (slug line) for a *master scene*. That master scene may (or may not) contain more than one *mini scene* or *beat of action*. The best explanation of what I mean is best illustrated through an example.

In the example below, I will first write the master scene heading, specifying the camera placement, the *prime location*, and the time of day.

Within this prime location, there will be other locations, each representing a mini scene or beat of action. I will not need a full master scene heading for those mini scenes. Instead, I will use *secondary headings*. Ready?

```
INT. MILLIE'S HOUSE - NIGHT

Millie steps in and shuts the door.  In a
flash, she races up the stairs and into

THE LONG HALL

where she suddenly slows her pace,
noticing a dim yellow light spilling under
the bedroom door.
```

```
IN THE BEDROOM

Bart waits nervously, clenching his .38
special in his hand.

IN THE HALL

Millie stares at the doorknob for a slow
moment -- calculating -- then quietly
opens the door.
```

Of course, the above master scene (containing all the little mini-scenes) will continue until we change the camera placement, the prime location, or the time of day. At that point, we will begin a new master scene with a new master scene heading.

Many writers triple space between master scenes, and that's fine. But you do not need to triple space between the mini scenes.

SLUG LINES

QUESTION
Why do you use the terms *master scene heading* and *secondary heading* instead of *slug line* like everyone else.

ANSWER
I get asked that all the time. I do it because there are two kinds of headings that *head* scenes, and I want to be clear to my readers as to which is which. May your scenes be masterful.

SUBLIMINAL SCRIPTWRITING

QUESTION
There is a sequence in my screenplay where there are flashes of

images, like TOM IN A CHAIR, TOM IN MOTEL ROOM, TOM DEAD IN THE ALLEY--quick flashes in an almost subliminal fashion. How would I format this?

ANSWER
The "flashes" are either subliminal or they are not. Just write what we see. There are many ways to handle this. Consider using the SERIES OF SHOTS if the flashes tell a little story; in other words, if they outline a narrative. Use the MONTAGE if these flashes revolve around a concept, such as passage of time.

```
SERIES OF SHOTS - TOM'S DEATH

A) Tom sits in a chair--silent.

B) Tom paces in a motel room, then glances
towards the door.

C) Tom lies dead in an alley.
```

If these must be quick flashes to get the right effect, then use the following:

```
SERIES OF QUICK FLASHES

-- Tom sits in a chair.

-- Tom paces in a motel room.

-- Tom lies dead in an alley.
```

SCHOOL DAYS

QUESTION
Within my script, the main character walks to and from school several times. I've established him leaving his house (EXT.

JOSH'S HOUSE) and arriving at school (EXT. LINCOLN HIGH SCHOOL). What about the journey between the two locations? Generally, nothing happens along the way (no actions or dialogue). How do I write this? Do I refer to it as "EXT. ROUTE TO SCHOOL"? Or do I mention it at all?

ANSWER
If you have read my column with any regularity, you know that the answer to half the questions I receive is "Write what we see." And that's the case here. Apparently, we don't see the route between home and school, so write something like this.

```
EXT. JOSH'S HOUSE - DAY

Josh exits the house throwing on his
backpack jammed with books. He rushes
through the front yard to the road.

EXT. LINCOLN HIGH SCHOOL - LATER

Josh arrives on the school grounds.
```

NOISES OFF

QUESTION
I noticed in a produced spec script that the writer only capitalized sounds that really exploded with description. For example: Tires CRACKLED across the broken glass. In other cases, the writer did not capitalize sounds at all. Is this something new? Or is it all discretionary?

ANSWER
Yes and yes. The current trend is towards *not* capitalizing sounds. However, many writers still capitalize very important sounds. It's at your discretion, but there is no longer any

requirement to capitalize sounds in a spec script. I hasten to add that every agent and producer has his or her own preferences, but the above is generally true.

LET'S ESTABLISH ONE THING

QUESTION
I have searched all the books and cannot seem to find the right camera angle/direction for this shot. I have an establishing shot focusing on a parade. The camera must rise above the parade to an aerial shot of the city. The camera will move over the city and lower to the main location in the film. The film begins in the present and immediately flashes back to 1974. The aerial shot is used as a time transition. What do you suggest?

ANSWER
The reason you are having difficulty finding this camera direction is because it is not used in spec scripts.

I assume you are writing a script on spec and that you have not been paid to write it. If so, you want to *avoid* camera angles and editing directions. That doesn't mean you can't direct the camera *without* camera directions. If you absolutely must have this shot, just write it out in narrative description.

```
We move up from the parade and over the
city until we descend into Central Park.
```

Just write it as simply as that.

The reason most producers and agents react negatively to camera directions is because your job is to write the story, not direct the movie.

THE FIRST CUT IS THE DEEPEST

QUESTION
Do you really believe that using "cut to" in your spec scripts really hurts your chance of being taken seriously? And if so, why do I see CUT TO throughout every script I read? For example, look at THE CONVERSATION by Coppola.

ANSWER
Let's take the second question first. Virtually every script available for purchase is a *shooting script*, but you are writing a *spec script*. Don't assume spec style is the same as shooting style (which is filled with technical directions). It is extremely difficult to get your hands on a sold spec script--they are rare. So I'm guessing that the scripts you are referring to are shooting scripts.

Also, writers who also direct or produce don't have to please anyone but themselves. You ought to see a Woody Allen script--it's not even close to correct format.

Now, the first question. Obviously, if your script is wonderful, but contains a few CUT TOs, it is not going to be rejected. But readers, agents, and producers who read dozens of scripts a week will glance through a script (before they begin reading it) to see if it is in spec format. The little things add up to make a good or bad first impression. Just one thing is not going to make a difference. But if you know better, why push it?

As an additional comment, not every Hollywood type reacts the same way. There are probably many who are not that focused on form and could care less. But generally, people look at scripts the same way you and I look at the want ads--they're seeing how many they can eliminate or screen out immediately.

DO YOU HEAR WHAT I HEAR?

QUESTION
If a hearing-impaired character has dialogue in the form of sign language, what is the proper format for writing it?

ANSWER
If the character uses sign language, then that is action and not dialogue. The question is how do you convey the meaning of that sign language to the audience? Well, it's hard to imagine subtitles for sign language, except maybe in a comedy. The only remaining option is to have a character interpret that sign language for another character in the scene, and that interpretation would be dialogue.

TO MONTAGE OR NOT TO MONTAGE

QUESTION
According to a recent article, alphabetically listing montage shots has become passe in spec scripts. If so, what is the correct format?

ANSWER
First, it never was correct format to alphabetically list MONTAGE shots. That is only done with the SERIES OF SHOTS device. (As a reminder, use the MONTAGE to communicate a concept, such as passage of time, and use the SERIES OF SHOTS for a narrative. Also, keep in mind that these two devices are often used interchangeably.) Here's what a MONTAGE should look like.

```
MONTAGE - DELBERT AND EDITH FALL IN LOVE

-- They share a picnic at the park.
```

```
-- Delbert jumps up and shrieks when the
ants get him.  Edith laughs.

-- They row a boat across a lake.  Delbert
stands to sing and falls into the lake.
Edith laughs.

-- They change the oil of Delbert's rusty
Ford Farlane.  Delbert paints his face
with oil--it's war paint--and dances and
whoops around the car.  Edith laughs.
```

You get the idea. Although it's true that you should use the MONTAGE sparingly, it has not yet been banned.

STACKING ACTIONS

QUESTION
Can I "action stack" for selected scenes and use a [traditional] narrative style for others, or do I have to be consistent throughout my screenplay?

ANSWER
You can combine styles, but don't use one style (action stacking, for example) just once in a screenplay.

For those who are wondering, *action stacking* is... well... "stacking" short sentences that describe action without double spacing between those sentences. Here's an example.

```
Bart spins around.
A truck speeds towards him.
Bart dives for the gutter.
Looks up a pair of legs.
The leggy woman looks down.
She has a gun.
```

Personally, I'm not a big fan of action stacking and I don't see it a lot, but it's perfectly legal to use. However, if you use it, show some consistency of writing style throughout your screenplay.

SPACING OUT

QUESTION
Regarding triple spacing prior to new master scenes, if I have a continuous sequence that involves different locations, should I still triple space for new scenes that are in that sequence?

ANSWER
You do not need to triple space at all. It is optional. Some people like to triple space between master scenes, and that's okay, but not required.

Again, to explain, a *master scene* takes place in a master location. For example, perhaps you open a scene with INT. SMITH HOUSE - DAY. If you then cut to the BEDROOM in that house, and then the DEN, and then the WINE CELLAR, those locations are all part of the larger location (the house), so we are still within the same master scene.

As you know, you normally double space between scenes. But, as an option, you can triple space before master scene headings, but not before scene headings within a master scene.

FOLLOW-UP QUESTION
Should I triple space if I use a new master scene heading to establish a second location for an intercut telephone conversation?

ANSWER
I suggest that you double space to maintain a sense of continuity.

A SUPER QUOTE

QUESTION
How does one present a quote or an introductory piece of text at the very beginning of the film? A SUPER does not seem quite right, since the text is over a black screen.

ANSWER
Just SUPER (superimpose) the quote, text, prologue, or roll-up over the black screen. And after typing

```
SUPER THE QUOTE:
```

double space, and indent ten spaces for the quote--just as you would for dialogue.

POTTY TALK

QUESTION
Is profanity and the f-word allowable in spec script dialogue, or is that something for the actors to add?

ANSWER
You want a little less profanity and vulgarity in the screenplay than you would find in the eventual movie. I have heard this advice from many agents and producers.

Of course, virtually everything is "allowable" in a screenplay, including profanity. It all depends on the market you are writing for, so my advice is to look carefully at the market you are writing for.

GETTING ANIMATED

QUESTION
I am working on a script for a film that would contain several
short animated segments. How should these be worked into the
script? Is there a standard format for this?

ANSWER
Handle it just the way you'd handle a DREAM or FLASHBACK
or MONTAGE that you need to work into the script. Here's one
possible way:

```
ANIMATION -- SILLY BILLY MEETS THE MONKEY
MAN
```

And then describe your scene or sequence of shots, just as you
would with a MONTAGE or DREAM SEQUENCE.

We often forget that there are basic principles behind formatting.
These aren't just a bunch of arbitrary rules. So don't be afraid to
extrapolate from some known principle if you come up with a
new screenwriting situation. What if the above were a dream
sequence? Handle it like this.

```
DREAM -- SILLY BILLY MEETS THE MONKEY MAN
```

or

```
EXT. AMAZON JUNGLE - DREAM
```

```
Silly Billy and his friends hike the
jungle trail.  Suddenly, the Monkey Man
drops out of a tree.
```

...And so on.

What if you have an animated dream? Just call it that, an ANIMATED DREAM.

If you have a particularly long FLASHBACK, DREAM, MONTAGE, SERIES OF SHOTS, or ANIMATED SEQUENCE--just label it. For example:

```
DREAM SEQUENCE
```

And then write out all of the scenes in the sequence, just as you would normally write scenes, and then end the sequence with this:

```
END OF DREAM SEQUENCE
```

Or, you could label each scene with an appropriate suffix.

```
EXT. JUNGLE - DAY - DREAM SEQUENCE
```

```
EXT. MOUNTAIN TRAIL - CONTINUOUS - DREAM
SEQUENCE
```

Just apply fundamental formatting principles. As screenwriters, we must understand formatting to fully understand spec writing. This is something I really get animated about.

THIS IS MY CHARACTER

QUESTION
How detailed should I be with the appearance of a new character? Do I describe only those with speaking parts? Do I describe past circumstances, such as "Josh's father left when Josh was just a baby," or "Kelly's sister Sharon is far more outgoing and, as a newspaper editor, loves to dig for the dirt."

ANSWER
First, let's set up the ground rules.

Rule #1:   You can only describe what we (the audience; the reader) actually see and actually hear in narrative description. Occasionally, you can cheat a little in character descriptions, but don't go so far as to tell us someone's history as a character introduction.   Don't write something like *Jenny used to be a cocktail waitress and had an affair with Jane's husband just a year ago, although Jane doesn't know it yet.*   You cannot do that because it cannot appear on the silver screen, but you can say that Mark is Jenny's wife or that Jane is Jenny's sister--you can probably get away with that.

Rule #2:   With character descriptions, focus on *character* and make the description visual in some way.   My favorite example is this: *She wears clothes that are too young for her, but gets away with it.*   Do you see that the description is visual, but that it also says something about her *character*?   That's what you want to strive for.

Okay, now let's answer your questions above.

I'll answer the second question first.   Characters without speaking parts do not necessarily need an introduction. However, you want every character to be clearly visualized by the reader.

For minor characters, you can do that with just a few words that makes the reader see them.   For example, "He's proud of his pony tail" (it's visual and says something about his character) or "wearing a Metallica tee-shirt" (it's visual and says something about his character).

For characters with speaking parts, it is even more important to give them some handle that the reader can grab them with.

Here's a description of a character from SCREAM:

```
BILLY LOOMIS, a strapping boy of
seventeen.  A star quarterback/class
president type of guy.  He sports a smile
that could last for days.
```

Now, the writer doesn't say that Billy is class president or star quarterback, just that he is that type of guy. The description is visual and says something about his character.

Also, note that there is no driver's license description of Billy Loomis. The writer doesn't mention height, weight, eye color, or hair color. Why? Because it's not important to the story. Only mention those physical details when it is crucial to the story. Instead, focus on character.

WHO'S ON FIRST?

QUESTION
In the screenplay I am working on, I have a sequence where the camera is the character's eye. During this sequence, the story is told in first person. I would be interesting in knowing how to insert this sequence into a screenplay written in third person without [using] technical intrusions.

ANSWER
When you say the "story is told in first person," I assume you mean that the character (whose eye is the camera) talks to or describes what he/she is sees. Thus, that character's *viewpoint* dominates in that scene. However, the narrative description would still be written in third person. Narrative description is always written in third person, present tense language. (First person would involve the use of the pronouns "I" or "me." Second person would use "you." And third person would use

"he," "she," "they," and so on.)   The fact that the eye is the camera changes nothing in terms of how you write description and dialogue.

That leaves the issue of communicating to the reader that the "camera is the character's eye." I assume that you mean that the camera takes the point-of-view of the character--what he/she sees, we see. You are right to want to write this without the camera directions, if possible. In cases like this, we are all tempted to write something like the following:

```
POV JANE -- A man walks towards her.
```

You can (and should) write the same thing without the camera direction, as follows:

```
Jane sees a man walking towards her.
```

(Incidentally, both examples are written in third person, present tense.)

Of course, if everything in the entire scene is seen from Jane's point-of-view, you could simply begin the scene with a note.

```
(NOTE:  Everything we see in this scene is
from Jane's point-of-view, as if her eye
is the camera.)
```

Yes, I realize that such a note is an intrusion on the story, but a rare intrusion is permissible if it clearly explains something that is important to the story.

Of course, that begs the question, How important is this POV stuff to the story? If you are just dressing up the scene for effect, you might be making a mistake. Your job is to tell the story in clear, visual terms, not direct the movie.

THE LITTLEST ORPHAN

QUESTION
I have been taught to never leave a slug line [heading] or character cue as an "orphan"; that is, never leave any of these as the last item on the bottom of the page. Does this also apply to "direction" [parentheticals; actor's instructions]?

ANSWER
You are correct all the way around. Do not end a page on a slug line, character cue, or parenthetical. Just move those to the top of the next page.

S-S-STUTTERING AND D-D-DIALECTING

QUESTION
I am writing a screenplay where the main character stutters almost all the time. How should I indicate that in the dialogue? I find it annoying to indicate it in parenthesis before every line of dialogue, so I came up with something like the following:

>   JOHN
>   W-what?   I-I d-don't
>   understand.

Do you have any suggestions?

ANSWER
Just show a flavor of stuttering; that is, occasional stuttering to remind us that this character stutters. Don't overdo it or, as you rightly said, the reader will be annoyed. Also, when you first introduce the character, indicate that he/she stutters.

The same holds true for accents and dialects--just give us a flavor. Don't adjust the spelling of every word to show precisely how each and every word would be pronounced in a certain dialect or with a certain accent. It will be too difficult to read.

HOW LONG IS TOO LONG?

QUESTION
How long should a [spec] screenplay be?

ANSWER
About 100-110 pages, but certainly not more than 120 pages. Ideally, a comedy will come in at about 100 pages and a drama or action story at 105-110. The minimum is 90. These are just guidelines, not hard-fast rules. An MOW (movie-of-the-week script) should come in at around 100-105 pages.

You may wonder why the 110-page limit when you've seen produced screenplays that are much longer than that. In virtually every case, those long screenplays were developed within the system; they were not spec screenplays.

The central theme that runs through this issue's column is to make your spec screenplay an "easy but fascinating read."

LOOK WHO'S TALKING

QUESTION
What is the proper format to use for an animal that makes animal sounds, but who also talks?

For example: A dog barks, then in a human voice says, "Hey, cut that out!"

ANSWER
Animal sounds should be written as narrative description. That's because only words are considered to be dialogue. Thus, you would write your example as follows.

```
Sparky barks, then speaks in English.
```

>   SPARKY
>   Hey, cut that out!

I SCREAM, YOU SCREAM

QUESTION
How does one write non-conversational vocal sounds, like screams? Are they written as action [narrative description]? Or are they placed under a character's name [as in the example below]?

>   LORI
>   (screams)

ANSWER
Write screams and human sounds (other than speech) as narrative description. The following is correct.

```
Lori screams.
```

Notice that I did not write the sound (screams) in CAPS. You may CAP important sounds if you wish, but it is no longer necessary in spec writing.

PARENTHETICAL ACTION

QUESTION
I have been told that I cannot end a dialogue block with an action
as shown below. Is that true?

```
                    GERTIE
       I'm going to make you hurt.
            (smiling with
            devilish delight)
```

ANSWER
You have been told correctly. You should not end a dialogue
block with an action. You can handle this situation in one of two
ways.

```
                    GERTIE
            (smiling with
            devilish delight)
       I'm going to make you hurt.
```

Or--

```
                    GERTIE
       I'm going to make you hurt.
```

She smiles with devilish delight.

DIALOGUE IS DIALOGUE

QUESTION
I have a scene where a character discovers a journal and reads an
entry from it. Since it's not really up to me whether the character
reads the entry aloud or if the actual entry is displayed on screen,
how should I format this in the script?

ANSWER

Before I answer the question, let me make two points. First, don't be ambiguous in a screenplay. Write what we see and hear. Either the character reads the journal out loud or the audience reads it silently--you decide in the screenplay. Yes, the director may change what you wrote later, but at least give him or her a vision of what *you* see.

Second, only dialogue is dialogue. You can only write in dialogue words that are spoken.

Now, in answer to your question, I see two ways to approach this formatting problem.

If the journal entry is very short, you might consider allowing the audience to read it. Use the INSERT for this.

```
INSERT - NATASHA'S JOURNAL, which reads:

          "I love Boris, but I plan to
          leave him for Fearless Leader."
```

If the journal entry is longer, then perhaps your character can read it to the audience.

```
Boris tiptoes into Natasha's room, spots
her journal, and turns to the last page.
His eyes soften.

                    NATASHA (V.O.)
          I love Boris, but his silly
          mustache tickles me.  I plan to
          leave him for Fearless Leader.
```

As you can see, all of this month's questions have to do with writing dialogue and writing action that is connected with dialogue. I hope your dialogue brings you a lot of action.

THE DREADED WRYLIES

QUESTION
Suppose my character joins the foreign legion and speaks in French, do I use the dreaded wrylies to explain that he is speaking in French? Or do I write the dialogue in French? Or should I use subtitles?

ANSWER
I've had legions of questions about foreign languages, so I am using the above as representative of them all. Even though I have addressed this issue briefly in a previous column, the time has come for a full treatise. First, let me explain the question.

The writer refers to "dreaded wrylies." Wrylies are the parentheticals that sometimes appear before dialogue speeches. The term developed because so many novice writers used the term "wryly" to describe their characters' dialogue. For example:

```
                SAM
         (wryly)
   And when you lay down tonight,
   remember to fall asleep.
```

And so the term *wryly* was born. The reason they are "dreaded" is because writers are encouraged to use them sparingly. Only use a *wryly* when the subtext of the dialogue is not otherwise clear. You may also use them to describe small actions that can be described in two or three words, such as *lighting his cigar* or *smiling wistfully*.

Using foreign languages
In working with other languages, realize there is one general rule: write your script in the language of the eventual reader so

that he/she knows what is going on. In other words, avoid writing dialogue in a foreign language.

If a character speaks in French, do not write out the dialogue in French unless the eventual reader is French, or in the extremely rare case that the meaning of the words don't matter. Simply write the lines as follows:

```
                    JEAN-MARC
                  (in French)
          Come with me to the Casbah.
```

Now the observant reader is likely to say, "But Dave, the word 'Casbah' is a French word." Yes, however it's also an English word with French and African roots, but the observant reader brings up a good point.

Instead of having your character speak in French, consider sprinkling his/her dialogue with French words to give us the flavor of French. Then everyone knows what is being said.

Now, suppose your character absolutely, positively must speak in a foreign language. Your desire is for something realistic, such as the Italian spoken in *The Godfather*. You have five options, depending on your specific purpose.

1. If it doesn't matter whether the audience understands the meaning of the foreign words, or if you believe the audience will be able to figure our the meaning of the words by their context, then just write them out in the foreign language. For example:

Tarzan shouts at the charging elephant.

```
                    TARZAN
          On-gow-ah!
```

```
The elephant turns and stampedes in the
opposite direction.
```

Or write the words in English using a *wryly* to indicate what language the words will be spoken in, as follows:

```
              PIERRE-LUC
           (in French)
      Imbecile.  Idiot.  Retard.
```

2. If the characters speak in French throughout an entire scene, then make a clear statement in the narrative description that all the dialogue in the scene will be spoken in French; then, write the dialogue out in English so that the reader can understand it.

...But this begs the question: How will the **audience** know what is being said? They won't unless they are French. For that reason, this is seldom a viable option. If your character must speak in French and it's also important that the audience understand what is being said, then the solution is subtitles.

Subtitles
3. If you write a long scene where French (or other language) is spoken, and if you want English subtitles to appear on the movie screen while the character speaks in French, then include a special note in the narrative description, as follows:

```
NOTE: THE DIALOGUE IN THIS SCENE IS SPOKEN
IN FRENCH AND IS SUBTITLED IN ENGLISH.
```

Then, simply write the dialogue out in English. After the scene ends, write:

```
END OF SUBTITLES
```

4. Another option for using subtitles is to use our friend, the "dreaded wryly."

```
                MICHELLE
           (in French, with
           subtitles)
      I spit on your name.  I spit
      on your mother's grave.  I
      spit on your column.
```

The spittle flies.

5. There is one other option for using subtitles. Use this device only if the sound of the words in the foreign language is important; for example, in the case of this space visitor's language, the words have a humorous quality.

```
      ALIEN                SUBTITLES
   Zoo-BEE, Woo-BEE.     You're cute.
```

My final advice is to choose English whenever possible and give us a flavor of the foreign language by including a few foreign words and/or flavor of a foreign accent. So until my next column, I bid you adieu.

SIMULTANEOUS DIALOGUE

QUESTION
When two characters say the same line at the same time, how do you format that?

ANSWER
Here's the first of four ways to present two people speaking at the same time.

```
                SAM AND JO
           Huh, what?
```

Or you can add a parenthetical to make it absolutely clear.

```
              SAM AND JO
            (together)
      Huh, what?
```

Or replace the word "together" with "simultaneously."

Here's a third example that you can use when the two characters say the same thing at about the same time or when they say *different* things at about the same time.

```
              SAM
      Huh, what?


              JO
            (overlapping)
      Huh, what?
```

And finally...

```
      SAM                 JO
Huh, what?          Huh, what?
```

LOCATING THE LOCATION

QUESTION
If, for dramatic purposes, you cut to the next scene by using a stark image—BLOODY FINGERS, for example—would you do something like this for the slug line: INT. BARN BLOODY FINGERS – NIGHT?   Or would you just write BLOODY FINGERS, and then pull back and describe the situation?

ANSWER
Since BLOODY FINGERS is not a location, it would not appear in the slug line. You would probably write it as follows:

```
INT. BARN - NIGHT

Bloody fingers tremble.  They reach for
the barn door.
```

In the above description, I focus the reader's attention on the
fingers first, and then on the action and surroundings. That
implies that we open the scene with a CLOSE UP on the bloody
fingers, and then the camera PULLS BACK (or PANS) so that
we see the barn door (and barn interior). Thus, we present a
clear, visual image to the reader without using camera directions.

ACTION SHOULD COMMENT ON CHARACTER

QUESTION
I'm presently writing a script which involves a lot of comings
and goings of the characters. In so doing, I find myself often
using the same exit and enter lines: Charlie enters or Charlie
leaves. Would this method be too repetitious in the eyes of a
script reader.

ANSWER
Yes. Be more specific and concrete than "Charlie enters" and
"Charlie leaves." How does Charlie enter? How does Charlie
exit? Make it a *character thing* by being more *specific*.

Let every action tell the reader (and the eventual audience)
something about the character and/or the story.

```
Charlie silently slithers in.

Charlie staggers into the bathroom and, on
his third try, kicks the door shut.
```

THREE, FIVE, OR NINE ACTS?

QUESTION
What are your thoughts regarding nine acts versus three acts?

ANSWER
Well, a nine-act story still has three main parts. It has a beginning middle and end, just like a three-act story. Some screenwriters like to think in terms of four acts—each about equal length. They still have a beginning (which focuses on establishing story, characters, and situation), middle (mostly concerned with complications and a rising conflict, culminating in some kind of crisis), and end (the showdown and denouement). Shakespeare used five acts, and even when he was in love, there was a beginning, middle (Acts 2, 3, and 4), and end. Most TV MOWs (movies-of-the-week) have seven acts. The first act is the beginning, and the last two are usually the end.

Basic dramatic structure is about the same for everyone. Now, how you specifically apply it to the content of your story requires some creativity and skill, and how you present the content of your story so that it is dramatic and compelling also requires some creativity and skill.

AND SITUATION COMEDY?

QUESTION
...But isn't a situation comedy just two acts?

ANSWER
Yes, it has a teaser, the first act, the second act, and a tag or epilog. However, it still has a beginning, middle, and end. The

way it differs from a screenplay is that the middle is divided by a pinch that is one of the following: 1) The funniest thing in the sitcom that makes us anticipate more hilarity while the commercial plays, 2) A very serious and dramatic turning point that makes us wonder what is going to happen next while the commercial plays, or 3) A funny twist that makes us wonder what is going to happen next while the commercial plays.

May what happens next involve a six-figure contract. Good luck and keep writing.

A PROFESSIONAL LOOKING SCRIPT

QUESTION
How unprofessional can I be in formatting? Do I have to have everything exactly right?

ANSWER
If your story is wonderful, then the reader will overlook many other things. Then again, the reader may never read your script if he or she is turned off by those "other things" when he or she glances through your script.

Obviously, the story is the most important thing, but formatting is important. In marketing, we call this packaging. Packaging is important in selling the product.

To give you a straight answer, if the errors in formatting are minimal, you will probably be okay. Keep in mind that different people in the biz have different ideas of what correct formatting is. However, if you follow the rules of *spec formatting* as best you can, you will probably be just fine.

HOW LONG A SCENE?

QUESTION
I've read in various articles and heard from a wide variety of industry professionals that a scene should take up no more than three to four pages (exceptions granted). How many times can this rule be successfully broken?

ANSWER
Any scene length is fine *if* it works. I usually recommend "challenging" any scene over 2-3 pages. Sometimes you need long scenes, but often you don't. There isn't a magic number, since it depends on the scene, the context, and what the scene accomplishes.

However, many scenes can be streamlined and improved if you will give them a hard look. For example, can you start the scene later in the scene without losing what is important to the scene? If so, omit some of the beginning. Are you being redundant in your scene? If so, you can do some condensing. Does your scene end strong, wanting us to see what happens next? In other words, is the scene compelling? If so, they you're probably okay.

THAT FIRST DRAFT

QUESTION
I tend to write the action for each scene as I visualize it "on screen." Sometimes formatting seems to get in the way of this creative process. Any tricks?

ANSWER
In your first draft, write it just the way you see it in your mind,

and use any format you'd like. Forget all the rules. Just get something down on paper. Write from the heart. Go ahead and have fun! Then, in your second draft, conform what you have to proper spec form.

THE OPENING HOOK

QUESTION
When writing my script, should I focus on catching the reader's attention quickly or on the quality and content of the story?

ANSWER
Both. That does not mean that you must open with a car chase and explosion, but you must pull the reader into the story.

RIGHT FIRST, WRITE SECOND

QUESTION
You say get the right or rights first before writing a sequel or adaptation, but my instructor says write the movie, then worry about the rights. Why different views?

ANSWER
My advice assumes you are writing to *sell.*

For example, let's say you write a sequel to the most recent Indiana Jones flick. Who are you going to sell your sequel to? Well, you can only sell it to the people who own the rights. And since they have you over a barrel, they can say if they choose, "We'll give you a grand for your script; take it or leave it." Do you see that you are in a weak negotiating position? Of course, if your script is absolutely brilliant, then maybe they will be willing to pay you your price. That could happen, so your instructor could be right. Just keep in mind that you have only one buyer when you write a sequel.

In the case of an adaptation, if you are already emotionally invested in a work that you have already adapted, and the seller of the rights senses that, then you place yourself in a weak negotiating position. My advice derives from my desire is to place you in a strong negotiating position.

AGENT RESPONSE TIME

QUESTION
How long does it take for an agent to respond?

ANSWER
Forever. Actually, it only takes several months. Give the agent at least a month before doing any kind of follow-up. During that follow-up call, ask when you can expect a response, and then wait until that time period has lapsed before calling again.

Remember that calling agents is fine, but the main thing is to keep writing.

SITCOM DIALOGUE

QUESTION
I want to write an episode for a situation comedy. Is the formatting for dialogue the same as in feature length scripts?

ANSWER
No. Sitcom dialogue is double-spaced and is different in other ways. Perhaps, a comparison would be helpful.

What follows is how a speech would be written in standard spec screenplay format.

```
                    GROUCHO
          The other day I shot an elephant
          in my pajamas.
                    (flicking his cigar)
          How the elephant got in my
          pajamas I don't know.
```

What follows is the same speech written for a situation comedy.

```
                    GROUCHO

          The other day I shot an elephant

          in my pajamas.  (FLICKING HIS

          CIGAR.)  How the elephant got

          in my pajamas I don't know.
```

As you can see, there is a big difference between the two examples.

One reason the TV sitcom style emphasizes dialogue is that a sitcom is actually a two-act stage play shot for TV. Usually, in a TV situation comedy, the emphasis is on dialogue, not on action. Often, there are only one or two sets for a sitcom series.

If you wish to write for a specific sitcom, you will first want to verify that scripts are being considered for that show. You will also want to see how scripts for that show are formatted. That's because there are slight differences from series to series.

EXITS AND ENTRANCES

QUESTION
Is capitalization of entrances and exits passe? Example: SHARON EXITS. I want to keep things "clean and lean," but can't decide if the CAPSs are a help or a burden to the reader.

ANSWER
Let me respond first for screenwriters, and second for TV sitcom writers.

In screenwriting, no CAPS are required for exits and entrances. In fact, you do not need to indicate entrances and exits at all. When a scene begins, simply describe the action we see and who is involved in that action.

If someone enters the scene or exits the scene, and it's important to point that out, then do so. But don't write SHARON EXITS. Doing so tells us almost nothing about Sharon or the story. Instead, describe how she exits to characterize her, or to reveal her feelings or attitude, or to reveal something of her character. Here are three examples:

```
As Sharon waves goodbye, she steps
backwards and trips through the doorway.

Sharon slams the door behind her.

Sharon steps triumphantly through the
doorway.
```

In a situation comedy, all narrative description is capitalized, and entrances and exits are underscored.

```
SHARON WAVES GOODBYE AND EXITS.
```

HOUR-LONG TV SHOWS

QUESTION
Is an hour-long TV show formatted the same way as sitcoms?

ANSWER
No. An hour-long TV show is formatted in standard spec script format, just like a feature length script. The only difference is that you label the teaser, four acts, and tag (or epilogue). Some hour-long TV shows are written in five acts instead of four.

Always get a copy of a script for the TV show you wish to write to see the formatting nuances of that particular show.

An MOW (movie of the week), by the way, is usually written in seven acts, but you usually do not need to delineate the acts in a spec MOW script.

SHOW ME THE MONEY

QUESTION
I heard the real money is in TV, but how can that be when some screenwriters make over a million for a screenplay.

ANSWER
Most established screenwriters are not making millions per script. But most established TV writers not only make six figures, they make it year after year. It is true that there is a lot of consistent money in TV writing.

The downside is you will work long hours to make that money. I have a friend who writes for a sitcom, who said he would love to take a break from TV, but he can't give up the big bucks.

Whatever venue you choose to write for, in order to make any bucks at all, you need to keep writing. Good luck!

IT'S STILL THE SAME OLD STORY

QUESTION
What is the difference between SAME and CONTINUOUS?

ANSWER
It depends on whom you talk to. Usually, the term CONTINUOUS is added to a master scene heading to indicate that it follows the previous scene without any break in time. Here is an example.

```
INT. CASTLE - DAY

Squire Hermagilde spots a group of Chub-
Chubs approaching the castle.  Scared
speechless, he lunges through the open
doorway.

INT. STAIRWELL - CONTINUOUS

He races down the stairs and through
another doorway.

EXT. DRAWBRIDGE - CONTINUOUS

He pulls the drawbridge chain hand over
hand, drawing the bridge up, just as the
Chub-Chubs arrive at the moat.
```

The term SAME is usually used in the same way.

```
EXT. STAIRWELL - SAME
```

Some people use the term SAME to indicate a scene that happens at precisely the same time as the previous scene; in other words, simultaneously. However, those occasions are extremely rare.

In summary, for virtually all intents and purposes, the terms CONTINUOUS and SAME are synonymous.

DAY OR NIGHT

QUESTION
I like to flow scenes together, and the suffixes DAY and NIGHT often become redundant. For that reason I try to use headings and sub-headings to avoid repetition of DAY and NIGHT. For instance:

```
INT. KITCHEN - DAY

Darrin heads out to the

BACKYARD

to find Ann resting in a hammock.
```

ANSWER
First of all, it's okay to omit the terms DAY or NIGHT from a heading *if* it's already obvious what the time of day is and *if* that time of day has not changed since the previous scene.

In your example above, the BACKYARD is not part of the KITCHEN, so a secondary heading is impossible. In other words, the BACKYARD is another master location that requires a master scene heading. However, you could end that second master scene heading with CONTINUOUS or SAME (instead of DAY), since one scene follows right on the heels of the other.

Therefore, this would be correct:

```
INT. KITCHEN - DAY

Darrin saunters to the door.

EXT. BACKYARD - CONTINUOUS

Derrick finds Ann resting in a hammock.
```

FOLLOW-UP QUESTION
In what situation could I use secondary headings?

ANSWER
You can use secondary headings when you cut from one (master) location to a location that is within or part of that master location. Let's borrow an earlier scene, and re-format it to illustrate this point.

```
INT. CASTLE - DAY

Squire Hermagilde spots a group of Chub-
Chubs approaching the castle.  Scared
speechless, he races through the doorway
and down the

STAIRWELL

through another doorway to the

DRAWBRIDGE

where he tugs at the drawbridge chain, and
pulls up the bridge just as the Chub-Chubs
arrive at the moat.
```

Since the STAIRWELL and the DRAWBRIDGE are both part of the master location (the CASTLE), they are secondary headings.

GOING UNDERGROUND

QUESTION
Much of my script takes place underground in a cavern that has its own continuous light, and time of day doesn't matter. In the slug line [heading], should I use DAY or NIGHT? Example: INT. CAVERN - DAY.

ANSWER
You probably don't need DAY or NIGHT for the situation you describe. One other situation that I can think of that's similar is OUTER SPACE. There's no DAY or NIGHT there, either.

SPECIAL WORDS AND ITALICS

QUESTION
If there are words in the action or dialogue segments that are unusual, such as the name of an extra terrestrial civilization called the *Barkuda*, or the Latin term for African lion, *panthera leo*, is it okay to italicize the words to a reader, so that the reader will know that the words are special and not typos? If so, would one italicize every occurrence of the word(s), or just the first?

ANSWER
Do not bold or italicize anything in a spec screenplay. That guideline may change in the future, but right now avoid those devices. Instead, if you wish, you may underscore special terms the first time they appear in the screenplay.

As a general rule, when you want to emphasize anything in a screenplay, such as a word of dialogue, or a sentence of narrative description, underscore the word or sentence. Do this only rarely. But keep writing.

THE NEW SPEC STYLE

This article was originally published by
The Hollywood Scriptwriter
www.hollywoodscriptwriter.com
PO Box 10277, Burbank, CA 91510 • 866/479-7483

There has been a lot of talk lately about the new spec formatting style. Throughout the 1990s, there has been a movement towards "lean and clean" screenwriting: Shorter screenplays, shorter paragraphs, shorter speeches, more white space, and the omission of technical instructions. It should come as no surprise that this gradual evolution continues to refine spec style. Let's take a quick look at where things stand at this moment in time.

The technical stuff

Let's start with what's forbidden. Do not write CONTINUED at the top and bottom of each page. Do not write "continuing" as a parenthetical when a character continues his/her dialogue after a paragraph of narrative description. Do not number your scenes. I realize this may mean disabling your software; that's because much of the available software is designed to format *shooting scripts*, while you (most likely) are writing a *spec script*.

Avoid camera directions: ANGLE ON, CLOSE ON, POV, PAN, DOLLY WITH, TRUCK, ANOTHER ANGLE, ZOOM, PULL BACK TO REVEAL, ZIP PAN, CRANE SHOT, ECU, WE SEE, and so on. Avoid editing directions: CUT TO, DISSOLVE TO, IRIS, WIPE. Notice that I use the word *avoid*. *Avoid* means to only use a technical direction when absolutely necessary to move the story forward. That's about two or three times in a screenplay. Remember, you are writing the story, not directing the movie.

MORE

In the past, when dialogue continued from the bottom of one page to the top of the next, you typed MORE (in parenthesis) below the dialogue, and then typed "cont'd" (in parenthesis) next to the character's name at the top of the next page. You still do. But only when you absolutely have to. Ideally, your dialogue should be so lean that you don't have to use MORE at all. Just move the entire dialogue block to the top of the next page or cheat a little on your bottom margin to get that last line in at the bottom of the page. (Warning: Do not cheat on your left and right script margins and dialogue margins.)

Parentheticals

You have read that you should use actor's instructions (parentheticals) sparingly, that you should not direct the actor in saying his/her lines unless the subtext is unclear. You've also read that since executives only read dialogue or just a few pages, that you should include some action as a parenthetical to help improve the read. There's truth in both statements. Let's be honest, executives are getting younger, often lack a creative background, and are asked to read more. The result is they read less. But readers (professional *story analysts*) read everything, after which they make their recommendation to the executive or producer. It's that recommendation that places your script in the running for a deal.

In view of that, continue to use parentheticals sparingly, but consider taking occasional opportunities to add a line of action (about 3-4 words) as a parenthetical if doing so adds movement to the scene. And don't be afraid to write brief description. Film is still a primarily visual medium.

How lean is lean?
Try to keep your screenplay within 110 pages. Paragraphs of narrative description should not exceed four lines. As a general rule, each paragraph should focus on an image, action, or story beat. Thus, paragraphs will often be only a line or two in length. Dialogue lines should not exceed 3.5 inches in width. Ideally, dialogue should consist of one or two lines, maybe three. (Yes, there are exceptions to everything.)

Author's intrusion
Generally, you should stay out of the script. Shane Black made "author's intrusion" hip. Here's just one example from page 91 of *The Last Boy Scout*: "Remember Jimmy's friend HENRY, who we met briefly near the opening of the film? Of course you do, you're a highly paid reader or development executive." Shane Black can get away with that; you and I can't. But having a personal writing style can add a lot to the read. I loved reading *Romancing the Stone*. The first line begins, "A size 16-EE boot kicks through the door...." I came away thinking that Diane Thomas had a lot of fun writing that story. I had a lot of fun reading it.

What *can* I use?
Use the MONTAGE, the SERIES OF SHOTS, the INSERT, the INTERCUT, the FLASHBACK (sparingly), and SUPERs. Use these for dramatic or comedic purposes (or for clarity or ease of reading), not to dress up the script. I have a copy of the original *Basic Instinct* spec script by Joe Eszterhas—the one he sold for $3 million. There is not a single DISSOLVE, CUT TO, ANGLE ON, SERIES OF SHOTS, MONTAGE, or fancy technique in his entire 107-page script. Only scene headings (slug lines), description, and dialogue—that's it. His focus is on telling a story through clear, lean, unencumbered writing.

The bottom line
Keep in mind that your audience is the reader of your script (not

movie-goers), and that he/she is weary of reading scripts. So don't encumber his/her read with technical directions. Just let the story flow like a river. That river will flow if you use visual, clear, and concrete language that directs the eye without directing the camera, and touches the heart without dulling the senses.

Finally, don't get paranoid about formatting rules; the story is the thing. Readers don't care if you indent 10 spaces or 12 spaces for dialogue, just so long as it looks "about right," has a clean appearance, and (most importantly) reads well. Hopefully, your lean script will earn you a fat check.

HOW TO TACKLE WRITER'S BLOCK

At last there is hope for suffering writers

originally published in *scr(i)pt*
www.scriptmag.com • 410/592-3466
5638 Sweet Air Road, Baldwin, MD 21013-0007

Few people realize that Writer's Block is a progressive disease that not only attacks the verbal processing lobes of the brain, but also debilitates the emotional response center as well. What starts out as a minor case of *idea retardation* can eventually deteriorate into *acute blithering idiotus*. The final stage of this horrible disease is *anonymity*.

Until recently, there was no hope. Now, recent research has shown that Writer's Block is actually a broad category of many related diseases, each with its own characteristics and symptoms. Identification of these specific diseases (or blocks) has made it possible to find a cure. If you have recently experienced any of the following common symptoms--finger paralysis, plot disorientation, or coagulation of the creative juices--then take heart! Help is here at last.

Autobiographicosis

This is one of the most common of all blocks. What makes this disease so insidious is the victim is often oblivious to the problem until it's too late and the script is rejected. Afterwards, the writer may recall a dull awareness of a flat and lifeless main character, or of a hero who is passive, perfect, and who has become an observer of the events of the screenplay.

At the core of this malady is the writer's past. His writing is so autobiographical that his characters have no life of their own, but have become mere appendages of the writer. As such, they can only act and speak in accordance with the writer's memories.

Once I read a script about a wife who was abused by her husband. The wife did nothing but complain for 90 pages. On page 100 a neighbor rescued her. The only reason I read this all the way through was because I was paid to evaluate it. I thought to myself, "This is often how real people behave, but movie people are willful and active."

The writer had painted herself into a creative corner. She was too close to the truth. She needed to use the energy of her personal experience and create a drama with it. Even "true" stories combine characters and condense time for dramatic purposes. She was suffering from *autobiographicosis*.

The cure for this condition is a radical charactectomy, or removal of the characters from the writer. The result is characters that emerge on the page with a life of their own--active, imperfect, and volitional. Sure, they may be patterned after aspects of the writer or of the writer's life, but they speak with a voice of their own.

In the early stages of autobiographicosis, the writer can be rehabilitated through a temperance program in which she learns to be close enough to her characters to love them, but distant enough to be objective and creative in her relationship to them.

Scribaphobia

Scribaphobia is characterized by a conscious or unconscious avoidance of writing the script. Writers with this disease would rather do the dishes than face the computer terminal. Often there is an underlying fear of not being equal to the task.

When scribaphobia was first discovered, it was widely thought that it was transmitted through casual contact with a computer diskette or even a keyboard. Now we know that this disorder, like all other blocks, is not communicable. Here's a progressive treatment that has helped thousands overcome the heartbreak of scribaphobia.

First, stop comparing yourself to William Goldman. In fact, don't compare yourself to anyone. You are unique and will make your own unique contribution.

Second, identify your fears about writing and courageously face them off, one by one. They will gradually shrink until you're in total remission.

Third, have a definite writing schedule and commit to it. Force yourself to write. Invariably, the first three pages will be crap, but once they are written, the creative juices will begin to flow.

An athlete never jumps into a major workout or a game without first doing warm-ups to work out the kinks and to prepare the body for optimal performance. Writing is no different. Try a few reps of letter writing to warm-up, or a few laps with a shopping list, or even the obligatory three pages of crap already mentioned. Once your mind is warm, it can more easily perform.

Chronic Ambivalence Syndrome and Museheimer's Disease

These two ailments are related because both deal with *toxic befuddlement*. *Chronic ambivalence syndrome* (or CAS) is nothing more or less than not knowing what to do next. In many cases, you may not need to know what to do next--just keep writing and trust the process.

However, if you are experiencing a loss of equilibrium, get feedback from a professional. Writing Groups can also help you in talking the writing problem out. Sometimes a seminar or a good writing book will help you gain the perspective and orientation you need.

Museheimer's Disease, on the other hand, is the false belief that there is a Muse assigned specifically to you who will come down from Olympus and whisper in your ear all the narration and dialogue for your script. The obvious symptom for this disease is suddenly finding one's self staring at a blank page or computer terminal for hours on end.

The problem here is not the existence or non-existence of the Muse. The problem is trying to write a script from scratch without first creating a premise, designing a core story with plot twists, and developing the characters.

Even then, you should consider outlining the story before you actually sit down to write it. This progressive, therapeutic approach will get you back on course in no time. Remember, you don't have to write the whole screenplay today, just a few pages.

Stuckitis

This is actually an advanced case of chronic ambivalence syndrome where the writer suffering from CAS lapses into a *stuckitic coma.* The way out? Mental concentration. The writer must draw on all her mental and analytical powers in trying to solve the writing problem.

The next step is to relax, wait, and concentrate on something else —badminton, pottery, anything. Meanwhile, the subconscious mind will work on the problem—this is the incubation phase.

It is followed by an *involuntary benign stroke,* an inspiration that usually strikes during a shower, at bedtime, or at some other calm moment.

The fourth step is a conscious evaluation or analysis of this offering from the subconscious. Once done, you may continue with your writing project.

Intrusion of the Inner Critic
If you've ever been in a creative fever and then suddenly found yourself correcting spelling and punctuation, then you've experienced this pernicious affliction which has blocked many a creative flow. To understand this disease, you must first understand how the mind works.

The mind has two sides, a creative side and an analytical side. Great writing presupposes the ability to alternate between the two sides. While in the creative mode, often called "writing from the heart," it is important to keep the "head" out of the way. And that's the problem. The analytical side often *intrudes* on the creative side. The cure is to teach this "Inner Critic" to wait its turn.

The key to the cure is to remain relaxed. Just brush these intrusions aside--don't give them a second thought. Tell yourself, "I don't need to get this right. I just need to get this written. I can evaluate it later."

When creativity fades, many writers induce its return by closing their eyes and visualizing the scene they are writing. Some listen to music. Others take a walk with a note pad. Anything to retain a relaxed but alert state of mind.

Preventive Medicine

Measures can now be taken *before* you are stricken with any of these diseases. First, end any writing session in the middle of something. Hemingway advised, "Leave some water in the well." By ending in the middle of a scene, paragraph or sentence, you make it easy to get back into the writing flow at the next session.

Second, realize that writer's block is an occupational hazard that every writer faces. When encountering a block, don't panic, just say, "Oh, this is normal, no biggie, I'll just work through it."

Third, trust yourself, trust the creative process within you, and trust the writing tools in your possession. Believe that everything is going to work out fine. Most of all, take the pressure off. Make writing fun, and you'll have fun writing.

INDEX

For information about Dave Trottier, his books and services:

Script consulting and analysis
Query letter analysis
The Screenwriter's Bible
Updates to *The Screenwriter's Bible*
Online courses and correspondence courses
Free screenwriting information

Visit Dave's web site, or contact him:
www.keepwriting.com
dave@keepwriting.com
1-800-264-4900

For information about *scr(i)pt* magazine or to send a question to Dr. Format:

www.scriptmag.com • drformat@scriptmag.com
5638 Sweet Air Road, Baldwin, MD 21013-0007
410/592-3466 • fax 410/592-8062